The Elephant on the Ceiling

How can we re-examine life and death through the lens of near death experiences?

Mike Hain

Copyright © 2021 Mike Hain

All rights reserved. No part of this book may be reproduced or transmitted in any form or by any means, electronic or mechanical, including photocopying, recording or by any information storage and retrieval system without permission in writing from the publisher.

ECMS Publishing—Aurora, CO
ISBN: 978-1-7365591-1-6
Title: *The Elephant on the Ceiling*
Author: Mike Hain
Front cover art: Caden Hain
Back cover art: Emerson Hain
Front and back cover graphic editor: Jason Disalvo
Digital distribution | 2021
Paperback | 2021

Dedication

These words are dedicated to every human who has ever found themself scared of the end....

There is no unknown....
The soul knows all

A soulless body is that of a capsule of nothingness.
It bends and breaks just as when it was alive
Its substance is not physical
Its true substance is somewhere else

— *Me*

We Need to Let Go

What if we all knew that this physical life wasn't the end? What if we all knew the truth? The truth that the transition from life to death is a continuous part of our journey and not an end. The controlling grasp we cling to would be gone. We wouldn't poke and prod the sick and death-stricken. Instead, we would sit with them and simply hold their hand and wish them on their way. We would send them on their journey and not attempt to tether them to tubes. Finally, our fear for them (this is actually our fear) would be gone.

There is one fact and one fact alone for every single one of us: WE ARE ALL GOING TO PHYSICALLY DIE. I know that is somewhat harsh but view that statement again. There is one specific word to focus on and it is not the word DIE. It is however, the word PHYSICALLY. Our body does expire although our soul never dies. The soul is as infinite as the universe. It only grows and grows and grows.

There is absolutely no reason for any fear.

Introduction

What happens when we die? Do we face judgement with the hopes of a heaven awaiting us? Do we reincarnate after adding or subtracting from our Karma card? Do we simply die and that is the end? Nope, nope, and nope!

Our physical death is just one of many transitions we will make throughout our soul's many lifetimes. When we pass over to the other side, there is no judgement from anyone but ourselves. We do reincarnate although we are not subject to a Karma-type level system. We either learn or do not learn the lessons we set out for in each earthly lifetime. If we do not learn the necessary lessons, we will attempt to learn them in another lifetime. Sometimes we need a do-over to get the necessary knowledge that we need. Just like when we are children and we don't always understand certain things the first time around. Lastly, we do not just come to an end after our physical existence; there is no end whatsoever. We are part of an infinite succession of life learning. There is only transformation from lifetime to lifetime.

Death is definitely the elephant in the room for many people. It's a subject that can be terrifyingly difficult to speak of or even think about. Death is a beautiful light of pure happiness and should not be feared in the slightest sense. I feel very fortunate in the sense that I have had an awakening of sorts regarding death. I feel as though I have had a near death experience without actually having one. This has given me an amazing sense of appreciation of life and death. A near death experience or an NDE is an unusual experience taking place on the brink of death and recounted by the individual after recovery. Many times an out-of-body experience or a vision accompanies these experiences.

I have begun to live my life from the viewpoint of someone who has had a near death experience (NDE) though I never have had one. Those who have had an NDE can be incredibly fortunate to have gained a beyond-life experience, an awakening. On the other hand, they have had to return to earthly existence which is not always an easy thing. The NDE and earthly life do not always compliment one another. Our brain accepts life because it is all that it has ever known. The brain has not experienced death and therefore it has difficulty with the concept. Our soul, which is the true essence of our true self, experiences the NDE and has experienced death many times throughout its existence. The soul embraces life and death. It understands the importance of both and can intertwine the two knowing that both are necessary for true soul growth. Although the brain collects memories that are catalogued in our soul, the brain and the soul are very different entities.

Consider the near death experience to be a kick in the ass or a slap across the head that tells us it is time to wake up. Wake up and start to live our life the way it should be lived. Everyone's wake-up call is different. Some people may not have appreciation for the beauty of their life while others may need to learn empathy, vulnerability, or many other lessons. It does seem that the most prevalent and beneficial lesson that comes from these experiences is to no longer have a fear of death. Almost one hundred percent of the interviews that I conducted and others that I have read made this very clear. Living a life without fear of death only provides comfort and never seems to cause difficulty in human existence. In fact, it usually aids the individual in having an enormous amount of appreciation for life. No matter what the lesson is, we need to learn it.

Many individuals who have had one or more of these experiences, report similar aspects of it. Some of these common similarities include:

- Seeing a bright light or complete darkness
- Coming into contact with a religious figure
- Being greeted by deceased family members or friends
- Traveling through a tunnel
- Feeling as though they are being pulled through a vacuum of sorts
- Traveling at an incredible speed
- A feeling of inner peace and all-knowingness
- Being in a blissful place with colors and sounds that are ineffable or unexplainable in human words
- Leaving their physical body and floating above it while being able to view everything that is happening
- Being told that it isn't their time and they have to return to their body
- Having a vision of their future life

- Having no future fear of death (in my opinion, this is the most important and easily the most common after-effect)

These commonalities can offer "soft" proof that these experiences are legitimate. People from all areas of the globe and of all ages and ethnicities have reported near death experiences. Although this is true, many individuals are just beginning to come forward with their stories. Many choose to not communicate their experience for fear of judgment from others. I spoke to many people that conveyed this fear. I was told by some that they had been ostracized by their family and friends for sharing what had happened to them. They were labeled as simply, crazy. This is a sad and detrimental fact for many survivors of a near death experience. Imagine having such a prolifically and impactful awakening only to be told by those closest to you that it didn't really occur. This would be a devastating response to hear; it would make me feel horrible if I were in their shoes. If you spoke to these individuals like I did, I believe you would feel the same way. Because of the true sincerity that I heard in each and every one of their voices, I take strong value in each and every one of these stories.

Obviously, we will not all have one of these experiences. The fact is that most of us could use a wake-up call though. How can we experience our own wake-up experience without a near death experience? To accomplish this, we need to step outside of ourselves. How can we each step outside of our daily lives and minds? We need to have a timeout from the grind of our nine to five lives. We live our lives in the fashion of, get this done and get that done. Run this errand and run that errand. We believe that we need to check off as many boxes on our daily checklist as possible. Yes, we need to manage our lives but this shouldn't be our main focus. We need to begin to focus on our life from our soul's perspective and not from society's. We need to turn our brain volume down and turn our soul's volume up. Turn up the love and the creativity. Turn up the empathy and the being in the moment. Turn down the entitlement and the societal expectations. These are crucial changes that have to happen to bring happiness to our lives. There are many ways we can achieve an individual and life-shattering change in our lives. We each just need to take the time to figure out these necessary changes and implement them into our daily lives.

In my last book, The Infinite Circle of the Soul: A Non-Religious View at Spirituality, I wrote a section titled Clarity from Chaos. We all have had, and I'm sure continue to have, chaos and struggle in our lives. These difficulties, although somewhat unsavory, are an amazing way to tap into a wake-up call. One of my favorite quotes I have ever heard is "lean into the sharp points." Don't back away and run from the pain and the struggle that you experience everyday. Lean into it and learn from it. Also, without struggle, we would have no appreciation for the great things in life. Can you appreciate a dark and starry night without ever seeing a bright, sunny day? Can you have appreciation for an amazing meal if you haven't ever had a bad one? I know that would not be possible for me. Ask yourself these types of questions and see what you come up with. So, please appreciate the struggle and realize that it is all about perspective. It's not that you were dealt a bad life. You were dealt the lessons that were needed for your soul to grow and to prosper.

My slap across the head occurred because I sat with the pain I was experiencing after my divorce. I felt every miserable and debilitating feeling that entered me and never allowed any of them to be pushed away or buried. I initially attempted to move on but the prematurity of this attempt quickly failed. I attempted relationships but I simply could not due to the fact that I was not healed. I was nowhere near ready. Believe me, I wished that I was able to but I could not. The painful feelings would surge through me like negative electricity with no off switch. The switch was always on and I learned to grow from the constant "on switch." This was the most valuable experience that I could have ever gone through. If you are experiencing a painful time in your life, keep your pain switch turned on. Think of your painful experience, whatever it may be, as a death of sorts. Learn from this death so you can grow and move on. The death that I experienced was what made me become alive. It's time for all of us to become alive once again.

Another way for us to evolve in our earthly life is to meditate. Meditation slows us down and lets us breathe, literally and figuratively. Wouldn't you agree that we all need to slow down? The world is constantly racing itself into exhaustion and it needs to stop. When beginning to do this, difficulties may exist. Clearing and silencing our brain is the toughest thing to do and typically the brain does not like to take a break and relax. It likes to jump from one thought to the next without us even realizing it. Try not to get frustrated if your brain won't easily allow the meditation to be successful. Just continue to practice and I promise you will be able to do it. With practice, we can raise our vibrational energy and get in touch with our soul. I highly recommend trying this practice. It may take some time to get good at it but once you do, you will be so incredibly happy that you did. This is the second way that I woke up.

Let's get back to the topic of death. Death can definitely seem scary. The thought that we will be gone doesn't sit well with most of us. Most people don't like the idea of things going away, especially when it is our own body that is going away. The thing is, it is only a body that isn't existing any longer. Our soul is not our body. Our soul cannot die, it simply changes form. I'm sure at some point in your life you have seen a dead body, possibly at a funeral or on tv. When you see that body, doesn't it appear to have had the essence drained out of it? Of course the answer is, yes. That essence that it was lacking was the soul. The soul is what gives our human capsule its life. It is the battery that keeps everything else charged and running. There is an energy to our soul that can never be destroyed, just changed.

Where does our soul go when it leaves our body? It goes to Source. Source is my term for Heaven or God. It resonates with me more so than the religious term of heaven or god. Source isn't a physical place just as the soul isn't a physical thing. It is an all-encompassing energy that is an infinite beauty that has always existed and will continue to always exist. We know that energy can never be destroyed, it can only change form. This change is the transfer from Earth to Source. Source is blissful perfection and it is whatever your idea of happiness is. Whether it is on top of a snow-covered mountain, a beautiful sunny beach, or soaring through the skies, your own unique Source is your own creation. Wherever you are truly happy, that is where your soul exists when you leave this life. A pretty comforting thought isn't it? An even more comforting thought is this: make your earthly life true and happy. Allow your soul's true happiness to lead your human existence to this same blissful life. That is what we all need to achieve.

Our soulful life, when we pass over to Source, has none of the stresses of our human life. No worries, no monetary issues, no anger or sadness, and definitely no disappointments exist when we are back with Source. Like I said, it's perfect. How is it that our soul is capable of this but our earthly life is not? Well, it is because of our ego. Our mindful ego lives within our societal existence and the pressures that are a result of that existence. If we could just let these things go and not make them the priority that we do, we would be so much happier.

Death is a break. A break for our soul to recover from the human life we just experienced. We, as souls, need a break to experience true happiness and reflection of how we lived our earthly life. Yes I said a break because that is what it is. It's usually not permanent. When we return to Source we have the time (although the concept of time doesn't actually exist there) that we need to heal. Even though we need our time on Earth and the lessons that come from our time spent here, our earthly lives are difficult and it takes a toll on our soul. This is why we desperately need this healing time. Depending on the level of difficulty we experience during our life can determine the length of our break.

When our healing is complete, we will return for another human life. We will choose the lessons we want and need to learn in the next life. We will go through conception and birth again and again. We will do this over and over again until our soul is complete. It takes many, many lives to become complete. Just like any major transition in life, we need time to complete it. When it is complete, we will reach enlightenment and we will be one with the energy of Source.

So is death sitting a little better with you now? I really hope it is but if not, it will be by the time you are finished with the book. Death is not the end, it is a birth. One of many births that occur on the path of our soul's life. It is one step of many on your path to pure perfection. Try to view your existence in this way: a path of lessons to achieve perfection. If you do, your unhappiness and human stress will ease, allowing for true growth and contentment. Try to be thankful that we each are allowed to live this journey and to have all of the amazing experiences that we do. All of these experiences shape who we are and shape our soul from a speck to a complete circle of enlightened bliss. Try not to run from life lessons no matter how difficult they seem at the time. Do not allow yourself to always focus on what is directly in front of your face, rather attempt to view the situation, or lesson, from every viewpoint. Learning to see the big picture is a very valuable skill to possess. Perspective takes practice for sure, but it will bring growth and wonderful wisdom to your life. After all, doesn't every conversation, situation, and experience have numerous sides to them? Of course they do so relish in the growth that comes from each moment of our existence.

To the well-organized mind, death is but the next great adventure. — *J.K. Rowling*

Death never takes the wise man by surprise, he is always ready to go.
— Jean de La Fontaine

The fear of death follows from the fear of life. A man who lives fully is prepared to die at any time. — *Mark Twain*

We all die. The goal isn't to live forever, the goal is to create something that will.
—Chuck Palahniuk

I have chosen to chronicle the subject of death by conducting interviews with various individuals who have had life-altering near death experiences. From the many interviews I conducted, I have chosen a handful to include in this book. Each one of these stories has its own uniqueness and individuality. I have chosen each one specifically because of the unique elements that I felt were important and relatable to all of our lives.

I will do my best to tell their stories in the manner that they deserve. They are all incredible in their own way and I could not be more thankful for these people and to all of the people that I spoke with. I hope that you can take away as much amazement as I have.

Part One
Razor Ray

One of the first interviews that I conducted was with a man named Ray. I knew very little about him, his life, or his story before speaking with him. When I go into these interviews, I try to be a compassionate and objective journalist. This interview, which became more of a friendly conversation, knocked me and rocked me to my core. Ray was not only inspirational, but he was engaging and infectious. I spoke to him for two amazing hours on the morning of Sunday January 10th, 2021.

On the other end of the phone I heard, "how you doing brother?". This was my introduction to Ray Reyes. He was so welcoming and made me instantly feel like we had known each other for a lifetime. Ray Reyes, a.k.a. "Razor" Ray, agreed to be interviewed about his near death experience that he experienced in 2013 when he was forty-two years old.

Ray was born and spent his early years in Texas. He was raised catholic and for the most part, had a positive religious experience as a kid. Although he sometimes found church mundane, as many kids do, he did like participating in the rituals. "I would steal my parent's car on Sunday to get to church while they were out. I liked going and after church, all my friends would ask me for a ride home. I was only thirteen." Ray moved to Michigan in the tenth grade.

His new environment was much different than his early years in Texas. This new place would be a new beginning.

Ray was a musician from an early age. Focusing on the guitar, he began to fulfill his musical aspirations. He had many bands throughout the years with many brushes with fame. Having Kid Rock produce and DJ on one of his band's records was just one instance of this. A second was recording and touring the world with the group Insane Clown Posse. He was living out his musical dreams.

Although great things were happening for him, he wasn't feeling like he had reached the top of his aspirational mountain. Having two failed marriages and an inconsistent musical career, he felt that his dreams were a farce. "It was a foreclosure of a dream," he told me. He felt like a victim from the failure he had experienced.

Years passed and time went on for Ray until one cold day in February of 2013; it was February 13th, 2013 to be exact. This would be the day that would change his life forever and would be, as he describes it, his "new birthday". It would be his day of enlightenment.

At this time Ray was in a serious relationship after his two divorces. He knew this time around would be the one that stuck. "We pinky swore that we would never get married." He had found happiness.

On that Wednesday, as he was laying on the bed, everything went black. The next thing he knew, he was on the floor sweating. With deep confusion setting in, all he could hear and focus on was his heartbeat. He could hear it pounding with every thump. As he lay on the floor, the girl he loved called for an ambulance. "She asked me, what did you take?" "I didn't take anything," Ray told her. "Initially, there was no pain but then all of a sudden a sharp pain flooded through my head." The ambulance rushed him to St. John's hospital. While he was there he began what he called, throat singing. This is a chant of sorts used as a form of musical meditation by many. He noticed that when he did this, the pain lessened.

St. John's could not accommodate his condition so he was sent to a second and then a third hospital. While at the final hospital, his eyes closed and they remained closed until something incredible happened. When his eyes opened, he was not in the hospital. He looked down and saw that he was standing in water and was wearing black Roman sandals. He was also wearing, as he puts it, "a white man dress." After noticing what he was wearing, he asked, "where am I?" The response he received was in song form and it was not the typical religious hymn or angelic choir. "All I heard was the Temptations singing, I know you wanna leave me. But I refuse to let you go."

"I looked to my right and then to my left. I saw enormous clouds but it was not cloudy. There was sand and a body of water. The next thing I knew, I noticed a huge mountain that wasn't there before. It just appeared. Carved into the mountain was the face of the Greek god, Zeus. All of a sudden, I saw the mountain begin to slide down into the water. When this happened, it created the most amazing and inspiring cool mist that I had ever felt." One of my favorite details of this story is that of an inspirational mist, so simple yet completely and spiritually complex.

"As I stared at this incredible mountain, I saw a very small man emerging from it. He couldn't have been more than four feet tall and was walking towards me. He was very pale with thin, curly hair and was wearing a white toga and had what appeared to be blue alien eyes that encompassed his entire forehead. This man looked like a cross between Frankenstein and E.T. He was almost Yoda-ish; he emanated pure gentleness. It's very hard to explain but there was a constant vapor motion in his eyes. At that moment I realized that the sky was his eyes and he could see all. I knew I was so tiny compared to this little man."

Ray was told by the small man, "you're not supposed to be here yet, but since you are here, let me show you around." He began to usher him around this beautiful place. He described seeing a man who was wearing red boots and tights skipping stones on the water. Ray asked the little man, "who is that?" The answer he received was, "you don't have to worry about that." Next, they walked through a type of threshold. From this new perspective he could see the earth and the sun. There was the most amazing reflection of the sun off of the little man. "You have a lot of people praying for you right now," the little man told Ray. Ray pointed to the earth and said, "I am going to share this story with everyone." The little man responded, "I know you will."

The next thing he knew, Ray woke in the hospital. His sister, who had never visited him before, was praying and crying at his bedside. He shouted, "I was just with God!" Her reaction was that of surprise and a little confusion but she was just happy he was awake and speaking. His doctor told him, "we thought we lost you there." He spent twenty days in the hospital recovering from the brain aneurysm and spinal meningitis.

After recovering in the hospital, Ray was able to return home and get back to regular life. A month later he was on his way to band practice. Although he was feeling much better, he was wondering how he was going to be able to pay for the mounting medical bills that were piling up. While driving, he asked God to help him with this financial pinch he was experiencing. He immediately heard, "go to the casino my son. It's all there for you." His first thought was, I'm not a gambler. Giving this message some thought he decided to go. Walking into the loud casino, he approached a craps table and began to place bets. To his surprise, he kept winning one roll after another. After spending a good seven hours placing bets, he walked out of the casino with $13,300. He could not believe this had happened. His prayer to God was answered. He shouted at the top of his lungs for everyone in the casino to hear, "you know who told me to come here? God!"

Throughout the years that followed, Ray has had time to reflect on his experiences. He realizes that he has paid a price for his survival. Since his "rebirth" he has lost his mother, baby sister, father, older brother, and god daughter. With the exception of his god daughter, he was not angry about these losses. He now understood where his loved ones were headed at the moment of their physical deaths. They were now in the wondrous and blissful Source. He did find himself asking, "why god, why did you take my goddaughter and not me? She was so young." The answer that he received was this: "people will begin to believe that I exist because of you."

Ray had one final loss not long ago. At the end of 2019, his partner of almost ten years and his niece were murdered in the very house that where they all lived. His partner's stepfather was living with them at the time and was very mentally unstable. One night, while experiencing a psychotic breakdown, he became enraged and murdered the two of them. He then left and committed suicide. The very woman that saved his life years earlier was now gone. This was yet another test of Ray's faith. He stated in our interview, "dark energy keeps trying to keep me from getting the truth out." He believes that nothing will prohibit him from relaying his amazing experience and what he knows is the truth.

The conversation that I had with this amazing man will stick with me forever. I have never in my life met an individual that had experienced so much amazement and so much heartache yet was so incredibly inspiring. Every word he spoke to me filled my soul with pure inspiration. When I hung up the phone on that Sunday, a feeling of trueness lifted me to an amazing level of faith. I thank Ray for all of his awe-inspiring words.

Our Own Huge Mountain and Little Man

I love the visions that Ray had during his near death experience; they were his and his alone. No one else will have the same thing happen to them. That was his own blissful and enlightening version of Source. What will yours be? Will it be a beautiful landscape or maybe a majestic figure of wisdom? We will never know until we finish this life. Our own individual and theatrical projection awaits each and every one of us at the finish line. Your idea of peaceful happiness is not the same as mine or anyone else's. This is a comforting importance in my opinion. The idea that we create our eternity is quite a beautiful thing.

I do believe that we each create our own earthly life and our life on the other side when we are between lives in Source. So many people feel that they cannot steer their life in the direction that makes them happy, however this could not be further from the truth. You are the one steering the boat. Now don't mistake this as controlling your life and future. We do not control our circumstances. We need to focus on our gut feeling when attempting to steer our direction. The best way, in my opinion, to view our gut is that it is our true self. It is our soul. Our soul holds our life map and knows the correct ways to maneuver that map. Now remember that we do in fact have free will to make the decisions that we choose, however we need to listen to our soul when making these decisions. Let go of your desire to control. Steering and controlling are two completely different concepts. My daughter said it best, "isn't it better to steer the boat than to control the boat?" Think of your life as a boat on the ocean. Can you control the waves, the weather conditions, or if the boat gets a hole in it? You absolutely can not but you can remain at the helm and steer the boat with all of your strength. Live your life always at the helm. I guarantee if you do, amazing things will happen.

After each of our earthly lives end, we return to Source for a well-deserved restful reflection. While we are there, our soul recharges and awaits our next earthly existence. I truly feel that while there, we choose our own reality. People ask, "is there a heaven?" One of my clients just asked me this very question. My response was, "yes there is but there is no hell." There is only a peaceful existence which involves a retrospective view of our past life. There is no damnation for our faults and mistakes on earth. After all, our earthly life is meant for us to make mistakes for the purpose of learning and to eventually reach a state of enlightenment. The only hell that could ever exist for us is one that we choose to create for ourselves. Our soul does not know hell. It cannot comprehend this humanly and negatively created idea. While on earth we need to focus on the positive and not on the negative. I know that this can be difficult at times but it is of the greatest importance. This focus will carry over when we pass on to our in-between phase. If we place our focus on positivity while physically alive, we will never attempt to create a negative and hell-like existence after we leave this planet. Your heaven or Source is whatever you want it to be. It is your soulful happiness. Mine is a snowy day at the beach with my kids. Yours will be.....?

Your little man has always been with you and will always be until the end of your earthly life. Your giant mountain is always in your peripheral view but to see it, you may have to close your eyes. You may have to look from your soul's point of view. Our physical view can often deceive us and guide us in an incorrect manner. We all have a blissful peace within us which is our true self. We just need to start looking for it. I started looking for mine a couple of years ago. At the time, I didn't exactly know what I was looking for. Honestly, I didn't even know I was looking for anything except an escape from emotional pain, but my soul sure did and your soul knows too. Listen closely to it and follow it wherever it takes you. It will take you to the happiest places you have ever found yourself in. Embrace this place and appreciate it for all of its beauty and knowledge and it will never disappoint you; I promise you that. You may have some painful bumps on this journey and that is definitely okay. In fact, it is extremely necessary for you to grow. I will say it again, "lean into the sharp points of life." Every emotional cut and bruise that you experience will eventually heal. The beautiful scar that is left behind will be a badge of honor. A badge that your soul craves and in the end, enlightenment is an enormous suitcase filled with these badges, badges of wisdom.

His Journey's Just Begun
by Ellen Brenneman

Don't think of him as gone away
His journey's just begun
Life holds so many facets
This earth is only one

Just think of him as resting
From the sorrows and the tears
In a place of warmth and comfort
Where there are no days and years

Think how he must be wishing
That we could know today
How nothing but our sadness
Can really pass away

And think of him as living
In the hearts of those he touched
For nothing loved is ever lost
And he was loved so much

Part Two
Toni T. Reese

Every single one of these stories is traumatic and heartbreaking in its own unique way. Near death experiences take an extreme toll on the individual that lives through it and also on the people in their life circle. No matter how tragic the situation is for everyone involved, an inspirational silver lining can be found. It may take some time to see it but it is always there. This silver lining can present itself in the main theme of appreciation for life and the lack of fear when it comes to death. Although many who have had one or more of these experiences may have difficulty returning to earthly life, they do attain a love for life. This leads them to living their life to its fullest potential. It also leads to a greater sense of empathy for others. Lastly, there is absolutely no longer a fear of death. Death is no longer an unknown for them and therefore is no longer a fear. These silver linings are amazing and beautiful. We can all read these stories and learn so positive lessons from them. Hopefully our appreciation, empathy, and dismissal of the fear of death will begin to exist much more within each and everyone of us.

The following story was by far the most difficult to hear. It is as traumatic as any story I have ever heard or read. The bravery that it took to describe her experience is beyond brave. I am honored to know her bravery and to tell her story.

The first word that I heard on the other end of the phone was filled with despair and pain. I have had challenges in my life but nothing would compare to the story that unfolded to me that day. With each word that was spoken to me, I could empathetically feel her painful tragedy. I could also feel her immense strength. I had always felt that I was a strong person but after speaking to Toni, I felt weak and beyond fortunate.

It was 2017 and Toni T. Reese was fifty-four years old. She had been raised by a Quaker mother and a Methodist father. Her mother was somewhat of a religious fanatic, eventually leading to her leave the church and pursue her own belief system. Toni always believed that there was some form of a higher power, although she could never understand the idea of judgement when it relates to being allowed into heaven. She always considered herself to be an open-minded person and gave her children the choice to believe what made sense to them.

Toni had been married for fifteen years. When she had met her husband, he had always been somewhat quirky and unique but they had a lot in common. They both were very intelligent people, as he had been a straight A student and was very high-functioning. He attained an intelligence level that could have been viewed as genius. She was happy and believed that they had a good marriage. It would turn out that there were many things that she did not know about her spouse. The happiness that she thought to be true was a farce. She would soon learn that he lived a secret life that was incomprehensible.

Sunday January 8th, 2017 would bring the truth to light. It was a typical Sunday morning at home and Toni was in her kitchen pouring herself a cup of coffee. Her husband walked towards her and put his arm around her. Thinking he was giving her a warm embrace, she did not resist. This assumption ended up being extremely incorrect. His arm wrapped around her neck and he began to choke her. With his other hand, he pointed a pistol to her temple. The next thing she knew, she was being dragged through the house and into her sewing room. The husband she loved and thought she knew was now someone unrecognizable to her. In this tragic moment, he had become a foreign entity to her. Understanding that he was a sociopathic and psychopathic individual who, as she would later find out, had done unspeakable acts throughout his life.

His parents, who were very religious people, kept their knowledge of their son's problems very quiet and believed that Jesus would fix him. They refused to further address his mental health and get him the help that he so needed. They did not want their family reputation to be tarnished by their son's psychopathic tendencies. They preferred to brush it under the rug and continue to live as nothing was wrong. None of this information was ever made available to Toni. His family completely kept her in the dark regarding his mental psyche.

Laying on the floor of her sewing room, she found herself immobile. Her husband had handcuffed her wrists to her ankles. As he sat on her back, he began to confess all of the truths of his life. She couldn't speak and felt completely helpless. Not only was she having to experience the physical pain that he was inflicting upon her, she was having to hear the horrible confessions of his unsavory life. The only thoughts that were passing through her mind were of her children. She glanced into a mirror across the room and viewed the reflection of her husband's face. His face "gleamed with pure madness," she stated. The thought of witnessing the person who showed you nothing but love throughout fifteen years of marriage, now exhibiting the craze of a madman is truly unimaginable.

As Toni lay helpless on the floor, her husband placed a towel around her neck and began choking her. He told her the towel was to "protect her pretty skin." These were the words of a stranger now, a terrifying man she had never before known. He had snapped into the terrifying madman that was deep inside of him. She knew that he would not snap back to the man she thought she knew. This second act of choking was not brief and she knew he had the intent to kill her. She could see it in his eyes and she could hear it in his voice. "This is it," she told herself. She knew that the end was near and she attained complete acceptance of her fate.

The brutal actions that were being forced upon Toni began to lead to something phenomenal. Suddenly, she was no longer within her physical body. In an instant, she found herself viewing the situation from above as her lifeless body was laying in an oval pool of blood and her bowels had evacuated. The next thing she witnessed was that he had stopped choking her. He had picked up his cell phone to make a call. He was screaming into the phone with a heightened level of manic anger. She could hear every word that was spoken. In his state of rage, he then threw the phone across the room and returned to her body. Sitting on her back, she could hear the sound of bones breaking; her body was at its end. Her soul made the decision to turn away from the traumatic scene. As she moved farther and farther away from the situation, she felt nothing but peace. There was no more pain or unhappiness. She turned to take one last glance at her physical body and that was it.

Toni had seen enough and travelled to a place of great beauty. She began to feel hands covering her. There were so many hands upon her that it was impossible to count how many there were. It was a gentle touching of sorts. There was no fear or discomfort in this place. There was only love. Along with the many hands that were comforting her, there was also a chorus of voices that continued to repeat the same message to her. "Just wait, be patient. Just wait, be patient." She didn't understand this message and was questioning what the voices were communicating to her. The next thing she experienced was a tug. Something was pulling her forward although she couldn't see what was doing this. Even though she felt this tug, she, at the same time, heard the word "no."

Toni could not view anything at this point. She was blinded by complete darkness. The only thing that offered some break in the darkness was what appeared to be many stars. She definitely did not want to return to her body. Trying to ask why she couldn't proceed forward, she was simply told to wait. The many hands covering her body seemed to be holding her in place, not allowing any further progression. The next thing she knew, there was a push on her face and a tug behind her. It was as if she was in some type of vacuum. All of a sudden she was back in her physical body. The extreme pain was back. She could feel every ounce of pain that had been inflicted upon her.

Although she was barely conscious at this point, she knew that he was moving her from the sewing room where the event began to a new location. She was placed in a different location of the house and left to die. After hours of lying helplessly, she knew that she had to somehow escape her captor. She waited for the opportune moment when he was not focusing on her. She miraculously mustered enough strength to exit the house. Toni luckily found her cell phone on a counter and headed for the outdoor cellar. Barely able to see clearly due to the trauma she suffered, she found her way.

Her husband had been up for two days and was in a state of delirium. This could have been one of the things that saved her life. He had laid down on a bed and she knew that he was in an altered state of mind. She thought to herself, "you got one chance to escape and this is it." She opened the door to the cellar and hid in the darkness. The sound of the door slamming awakened him and he raced out of the house armed with a gun. He randomly fired four shots. She knew that the gun held six shots therefore he had two remaining. She knew that if he found her, one of those bullets would be for her and the other for him.

As Toni sheltered in the dark cellar, she knew she had to call for help on the cell phone. Not wanting to make any noise, texting was the smart option. Her eyes were so damaged from the beating she could only see the glow of the light from the phone. Somehow her fingers located the text feature and she began to type a frantic message to summon help. Luckily, she sent the message to her close friend who contacted the police.

Toni was severely beaten and held captive in her own home for thirteen hours. She suffered such extreme abuse to her face that she was unrecognizable. She underwent two reconstructive surgeries to repair the damage and to make her appear human again. She suffered many broken bones and damage to her ear and breast. The recovery process was extensive and lasted for a year. Bodily scars left behind remind her of this horrid event on a daily basis. Due to the lack of oxygen during the choking, she has lost approximately thirty percent of brain function although she stated that her instincts are much sharper now.

Toni is a survivor. I knew the second that I heard her voice that she attained the strength of a survivor. That strength is one of the reasons she is still here today. Also, it wasn't her time to leave her earthly life. She wasn't given the choice to return to her body or to remain within the blissful state of Source. Her life would need to continue for the better good of her soul's growth. When asked if she knew why her life needed to continue, she simply stated, "I really don't know."

We don't always know what our true purposes are but they are always there hiding amongst the shadows of life.

How Do We Find Our Strength and View Our Life From Above

How strong of a person do you consider yourself to be? Some of us feel as strong as a bull while others have faced many difficulties throughout life that have led to a feeling of being weak. Some people have unlimited confidence while others suffer from extreme insecurity. We all need to take a deep look within ourselves to find our strength. Everyone has it within them whether it is lying right on our surface or buried beneath our own sight.

Strength occurs when we each attain the capacity to withstand great force or pressure. The force and influence from others upon us can deplete our strength at times but it does not have to remove our strength. Many social pressures exist in our earthly lives. You most likely feel them everyday of your life. I know that I have. Even though I have always been a person who resisted social pressures, there are still moments that get to me. I believe that a good way to lead each day is to think of yourself surrounded by a protective bubble. All of our strength is inside of the bubble and nobody can pop it no matter how hard they try. Nobody can pop your strength!

In the story of Toni, she found her strength within the tragedy that she experienced. Not only did she have to find physical strength, she had to find her will to live. Most of us will not experience anything like she did but we all can learn from it. The will to live can take strength for a lot of individuals. As we all know, life is hard. It is hard for everyone and that will never change but we can lead our lives from a different perspective. We can view life as difficult and feel that we have been dealt a bad hand or we can view these hardships as lessons that make us better and stronger. As I have said so many times, we do not learn from ease. We learn from challenges that present themselves on a daily basis. If everything in life came easy with a pretty bow on top, we would never evolve emotionally or for that fact, spiritually. Cherish these difficulties. These lessons can build our strength if we allow them to and only weaken it if we allow them to do so.

Aside from having the strength to live day to day and to learn our life lessons, we need to have the strength to not fear death. Every single one of us will physically die. This is a one-hundred percent fact. So many people have an extreme fear of death. It may be due to the fear of the unknown or the fear of letting go of our earthly lives. This fear can be crippling and debilitating for some. When we live in constant fear of anything, we aren't truly living. When we read or listen to the stories of people who have had near death experiences, we can begin to abandon the first of these fears. The unknown is no longer an unknown. The unknown is now known from these stories. We can have reassurance from the stories that all of these people have told. What we have thought of as the end, is not the end whatsoever; it is just a transition. A transition from physicality to a purely blissful existence.

Now the second of these fears, letting go, can be so incredibly difficult for many people. The inability to let go usually stems from the need to have control which in turn stems from fear. People have fears of life and fears of death. All of these fears can lead to wanting to control every aspect of life. I believe that the key to accepting death is to first let go of the fears of life. If we start to relinquish our need to control the aspects of our daily lives then maybe we can begin to let go of our need to control the end of our physical existence. You can attempt to fight and fight to stop death from factually existing, but that's a fight that you will not win. Death is not a brick wall that you will slam into, it is however a nurturing and freeing state of inconceivable freedom from the stress and pain of our earthly existence.

Many of these stories are beyond horrific and tragic but there is such a beautiful silver lining waiting for all of us to embrace if we can let go of our previous perspectives of death; let go of our previous fears. If your eyes are truly open, life as well as death is one big silver lining. Keep your glass half full of the beauty of it all and not half empty of fear.

When someone has experienced a near death experience, many times they witness their physical existence from a new point of view. Whether they are looking down upon their body, or in the case of Toni, moving away from it, they no longer are seeing from their physical viewpoint. They are not seeing themself from a mindset that has been tainted with social beliefs and judgements. They are seeing the bigger picture of themself. They are seeing from their soul's perspective, the true perspective. We all are a soul and not just a tangible human being. The soul sees much differently than that of our human eyes that are controlled by our mind. Our soul is our truth and is connected to everything and it does not attain judgement and never lacks in strength. It is purity at the highest level. That imaginary bubble that I spoke of earlier is our soul. It can not be penetrated by any negativity or fear. Your soul is what will always protect you and give you your strength. Never forget this. If you find yourself doubting your own individual strength, remember that your soul isn't doubting it in any way. Look deep within yourself and your soul will unveil your true strength that you are having difficulty seeing.

Fear Itself is Undefined
by Biance Flores

I lie on my bed, soaking my pillow with my tears.
I try to remember exactly what it is that I fear.
Is it the passing of time or the love that I lack?
Is it the mistakes that I've made or the fact that I can't bring the past back?
What is it that I'm afraid of?
Why am I so scared?
Is it the people I've hurt or the people who've hurt me?
Am I afraid of everything that I can't seem to see?
Is it the love of a friend or the loss of my family?
Is it the possibility that my life can end in a tragedy?
What is it that I fear most?
What do my eyes say I'm scared of?
Is it the sun that sets but won't seem to rise?
Is it the hope that I have that always seems to die?
Is it the trust of a person that I cannot begin to grasp?
Is it all the memories of my horrid past?
Is it me?
Can it possibly be that the thing I fear most is the thing I can't be?
The things that I try to understand?
The me that I try to be with when I'm feeling sad?
The person I'm expected to be? Is that what I fear?
I think the thing I fear most...is me.

Part Three
Carolyn Muncaster

I'm sure you have, at some point in your life, wished that you could view your future. I think we have all had moments like this. Having the ability to be witness to our future could be an amazing thing to experience. We could be privy to very valuable information that could serve our life in a positive manner. Such a vision of your future could bring a sense of peace to your life. It could bring a newfound appreciation for life that we can sometimes lack. In your opinion, would it be beneficial or debilitating? Would you want to have such a vision? This is a question that almost none of us will ever be able to answer. The following story does in fact answer this question. This is Carolyn's story.

Carolyn Muncaster was born in the early nineteen seventies and grew up in the Catholic Church. Her mother, who was at one point a nun within the church, had very strong beliefs when it came to religion. These strong beliefs were passed on to her daughter. Carolyn was actually the first female altar boy when she was young. She truly felt her own strong ties to the church and aspired to be a nun herself when she became an adult.

The first time that Carolyn had a close experience involving death was when she was nine years old. Her nanny, who she was very close to, passed away. The death had a very strong impact on her and she struggled to accept the loss of her friend and caregiver. One day she was feeling very distraught and got down on her hands and knees. She began to pray for some guidance to help with her sadness. While praying, she opened her eyes and witnessed a very bright light. This light was brighter than she had ever witnessed before. Within this amazing light she had a vision. Carolyn saw Jesus Christ sitting and holding her. He communicated a message to her: her friend and caregiver that she cared so deeply for was okay. Even though she was no longer in Carolyn's life physically, she wasn't simply gone. This vision and knowledge was extremely impactful for Carolyn as a young child. The comfort that it provided helped her immensely.

Fast forward thirteen years. Carolyn had become pregnant with her first child. She had a fairly difficult pregnancy and on Friday May 19th, 1995, at the age of twenty-two, she went into labor. She was experiencing severe swelling and pain and the doctors had no option but to perform a C-section procedure. She had a beautiful, eleven pound baby girl. The last thing that Carolyn recollects is holding her new baby and talking with her parents. After that, everything went dark as she began to hemorrhage. The darkness that ensued was lifted by a sudden bright light. The light that she was witnessing was getting larger and larger. In an instant, she found herself being pulled into this magnificent light. The light washed over her with an extreme calmness and peacefulness. She found herself hearing many sounds and voices that surrounded her. There were numerous conversations happening simultaneously and even though she could hear everything, she could not hear any of it at the same time. She was unable to decipher actual words coming from these voices. An ineffable audio experience if you will.

She had a strong desire to continue further into the light but something stopped her. All of a sudden she heard one main voice emerge from the many conversations. This voice stated one simple message: "You cannot stay, you have a baby now." This was definitely not what she was wanting to hear. She remembers telling the voice that she wanted to stay. The next thing she knew, she was viewing a vision of her future self. In this vision she was an elderly woman. "I looked down and saw many children. I knew them but at the same time, I didn't." Once again, the voice emerged and stated, "This is why you must go back. They need you."

Carolyn, in an instant, found herself back in her physical body. As she was recovering for some time in the hospital, she reflected on the vision that she was shown. The vision never became a blurry memory that she could not remember. She knew that this was definitely not just a dream. It was an actual experience that had really happened. Every single detail of it was deeply ingrained into her psyche. Although this was such a prolific experience for her, she never spoke a word of it to anyone for many years. The first time she ever told anyone of her vision was many years later when her daughter, Natasha, was in her teens. She decided to tell her daughter what had happened to her after she had given birth so many years ago. Her daughter was very receptive and they both were glad she shared this amazing experience. Carolyn never spoke a word of it to her mother for fear of judgment and dismissal of her profound vision.

When asked if this view of her future did in fact come true, her answer was incredible. In her other-world vision, she saw thirteen children standing around her. Having only given birth to one child, this didn't seem to make sense until she elaborated. "I have one child, three grandchildren, and nine nieces and nephews." Carolyn is extremely close to each and every one of them. She knows that her survival was very important to not only her daughter, but to all of the children in her life. Her impact upon all of them has made her life and theirs incredibly valuable.

Carolyn's vision definitely came to an earthly fruition and she is very thankful to have experienced what she did.

Having Our Own Vision

We know that most of us will not be given a view of our future life like Carolyn did, however we can give deep thought to our lives and attempt to steer our present life in the direction we wish to travel. Now some of you may interpret this as a need to control your life. This is not the message that I am conveying. I want all of you to use your free will and your gut to guide yourself into the future. Your gut is your genuine steering wheel. Your gut, also known as your intuition, knows the true direction you must proceed. Open yourself and become in tune with your gut feeling. I have said it before and I will say it again, follow this gut feeling. I'm sure that you have had times in your life where you felt you should or shouldn't do something but then your brain stepped in and did an override of sorts. I know that this has happened to me on several occasions. A few years ago I really started to listen to these feelings and did not let my brain step in and make the decision and you know what? Life began to be less of a struggle and much less stress resided within my life. If you do this, I promise that you will always navigate correctly and you will always fulfill your soul's true path. All of our futures should always be a focus, but we all must live our lives in the present and in the moment. Just remember to make each one of these moments count and accumulate to an amazing future.

Each and every one of us has the capability to make the choices that will lead to a fruitful future. Yes we will make mistakes along the way but that is okay. These mistakes lead to knowledge and experience that is extremely valuable. Allow these mistakes to create a syllabus that you can refer to as your life progresses. We all can refer to prior missteps when presented with a similar future situation however many individuals do not do this. They continue to repeat mistakes and do not learn from them. This lack of learning prohibits them from moving their lives forward in a positive manner. They tend to move in more of a circular fashion of negative repetition that leads to nothing but unhappiness and despair. This is a cycle that many people endure on a daily basis for their entire lives. These individuals need to take a step back and view this repetition from an outside perspective. This will allow for a newly-gained fountain of knowledge that will lead to positive changes that are necessary for living a happy existence. Knowledge leads to progression and progression leads to a happy life and eventually to our soul reaching enlightenment.

How do you view your tomorrow? Now this means your literal tomorrow as well as your tomorrow fifty years from now. We don't want to focus on the future so much that we miss out on our today, however we should always have it in the back of our minds. I have learned that when we experience hardships and turbulent times in our lives, we tend to dwell on today. This creates a sort of dark tunnel-vision with no hope of peripheral sight. This dark tunnel of today makes tomorrow even darker. Imagine yourself standing on a beautiful beach at sunset but all you can see is the very bright center of the sun. You would have no idea what you were viewing. You would not be seeing the entirety of the amazing landscape that you were standing among. That is what our own negativity basically equates to. It inhibits us from witnessing our own beautiful sunset (and trust me, we each have one within us). We become consumed with the negativity and lack the ability to see a positive future. I believe that these are the crucial moments that build strength within us and especially within our soul.

Seeing through the negative and difficult times in life definitely is not easy and takes practice. There are, however, coping skills that we can turn to in these moments; skills that will focus on the big picture which obviously includes our future. For me, I just have to think about or look at my children or sit down and write these books and it snaps me out of my engulfed negativity. Other coping mechanisms can be writing all of these feelings and thoughts down on paper or letting them out through creative avenues such as art or music. Whatever works for you, do it. Let it out! If you do not prefer to write, talk about it. Talk to anyone who will listen. This is crucial to navigate through the difficult times in our lives. Bottled up negativity and sadness are nothing but a time bomb that gets bigger and bigger until it eventually explodes. Please talk and don't explode!

We each can have our own individual vision for our future. You can create the vision that you wish for yourself. All that is needed is to look deep within and realize what truly makes you happy, that thing or things that make you smile. Focus on those aspects and your life will be fulfilled; focus on your smile. What is more important than a sincere smile? Nothing is more important than that. A smile can change your day or the people around you in an enormous way. A smile can literally change the world! If you find yourself living day in and day out without a smile on your face, it is time to make some changes. Your life is yours and yours alone. It is not meant to be made for other people and what they want your life to equate to. Your happiness is what is crucial. Create your own canvas of possibilities. Never stop painting your future; never stop creating your happiness. Everyday, make it a point to be as happy as you can be and make your life look exactly the way that you want it to look like.

Carolyn's Vision
by Mike Hain

When I was called, I gladly went
When the light greeted me, I was calm
When in the light, I was at peace
I felt an amazement

When I was there, I wanted to stay
When I was there, I could not imagine leaving
When I heard the voices, I tried to listen
I only heard one

When I saw, I was enlightened
When they surrounded my feet, I knew
When bliss engulfed me, I was happy
I knew them all

When I was told, I understood
When the need was presented, I agreed
When I heard, "They need you," I felt
I would then return

Part Four
Barb Merlihan

It is true that the stories I have chosen to use in this book are of near death experiences, however I did stumble upon one that was quite different. I have selected these stories very carefully and with great care for they are each individual in their own right. When I first heard from Barb Merlihan, I was definitely curious about her story. It was very different from all of the others and definitely very different from any I had ever read about.

She never had a near death experience though her experiences were very much equivalent to any I had known. Barb never died therefore she never had a NDE. After speaking with her, I truly felt that her experience was so unique and special that it deserved its own category. She had what I have coined as an ELE or what I have titled as an elevated life experience. When I ran this title by her, she was ecstatic. This story is riveting and as unique as they come. It is told with one hundred percent merit and had a profound impact on me. I hope that you learn and gain as much from reading it as I did hearing it.

I sat down that Saturday afternoon with my notebook and pen ready to record her story. I knew going into this interview that it would be much different than the others that I had conducted. Part of me didn't know if Barb's story would work for the book and the other part of me was so intrigued by it that I couldn't wait to hear it. Since her story was not one of a near death experience, I was wondering how it would relate to the book's subject. It related beyond measure.

The kindness in her voice drew me in instantly. I could hear the genuineness and sincerity with every word she spoke. For me, it was instantly a comfortable conversation. At sixty-two years of age, Barb was full of life and had a great appreciation for it. She spoke with nothing but positivity when it came to her past and present life. She has experienced so many amazing feelings and moments of synchronicity that I was in awe. Her glass was so full that it spilled over onto me like a warm blanket.

At the age of seventeen, Barb experienced three separate and individually unique moments of profound amazement. Keep in mind that all of these occurrences had no medical reasoning attached to them. She had a near death experience without the presence of death or any injury or illness. She was a profound anomaly among anomalies. Each one of these experiences took her further than the prior one.

In the first of these, she witnessed her own body from above. She was only seventeen years old and found herself hovering above where she had a feeling of complete peace and utter amazement. "I felt as if I was testing this peaceful feeling by attempting to conjure up negative words and feelings such as hate or anger only to find that there was no feeling attached to these words." There was a momentary need to question the marvel of what was happening. The next thought that crossed Barb's mind was that of her parents finding her dead and not understanding that she was okay. She was actually far more than just okay. In this altered state she was not dead or anywhere near the proximity of death though she was convinced that she was; so much so that she was concerned with being found in a death state.

The second experience that occurred was even more heightened in its level of profoundness. She describes it as much more universal in the sense that she was somewhere in the cosmos viewing Earth in its entirety. "I was with my sister (who is still alive) and we were laughing at how ridiculous and silly the whole experience was. It was as if on the earthly plane there was a total ignorance or misunderstanding of true reality." It seemed as though her consciousness was being privy to information while within this heightened level of reality. The veil was being lifted in these moments and a profound understanding was taking place. This understanding would remain within Barb for the rest of her life.

The third of these experiences was by far the most incredible. She found herself traveling very quickly through a tunnel or some type of space where there was a feeling of being enveloped. There was also a one-hundred percent absence of any type of fear of what was occurring. This is her account of what followed:

"I was greeted at the end of this tunnel by people or beings that were so kind and welcoming. The entire room was filled with these beings, however I didn't recognize any of them. At that point in my life, I hadn't had anyone close to me pass on. These beings, mostly women, were dressed in long brown robes.

They asked me if I wanted to meet God. They then prompted me to move towards a stage where he was. With my head down, I began to move towards this stage. I remember the floors being wooden and earthy and I remember feeling very comfortable in that room. I continued to slowly move towards this stage knowing that if I raised my head to look at God, that would indicate my decision to remain there and not return to my earthly life. This was a decision that was very difficult for me to make. I continued on further, head still down, reaching the steps that led up to the stage. When I got to the top of the steps, I saw the feet of who I assumed to be God. He were enveloped in an array of beautiful white and golden light. It seemed as though he was sitting on a throne and the light was the lower portion of a brilliant garment that he was wearing that laid across his feet and spilled onto the floor around him. It was absolutely glorious. I still did not raise my head to look at him. There was an intense ringing in my ears and the vibration got so loud and distracting that I soon felt reentrance into my body."

Preceding each of these experiences, Barb reported feeling something entering and exiting her body and that there was a vibrational ringing that could be heard. No matter how hard she tried, she could not stop these things from happening. It was as if she was paralyzed or frozen with no sense of controlling herself or what she was experiencing. Just as with someone who has no control during a near death experience, Barb had no control while having her elevated life experience.

The following day, she reflected on what had happened and she knew that none of it was a dream. She knew that this had been some "other worldly" experience and decided to begin to research what had happened and found evidence that this occurrence was in fact real. From that point on, Barb was spiritually changed. The truth that she had searched for since her childhood had finally come to fruition.

That was the first chapter of Barb's profound experiences. The second chapter came eight years later when she chose to communicate what had happened for the first time. The person that she confided in was her good friend Steve. The two friends had met while living in Georgia and working together. Though they were only friends, Barb believes that they were soulmates. Telling him in great detail of her experiences, he was not only intrigued, he was envious. His response was, "I wish that I had something like this to believe in." Barb simply replied, "someday when it happens to you, you'll say, ah ha this is what she was talking about."

Several months after telling her story, Steve was involved in a horrible motorcycle accident. Following the accident, he was resuscitated twice and did survive although he remained in a semi-comatose state for the next five years. As you can imagine, Barb was beyond devastated by what had happened to her friend. She would visit him and sit at his side day after day. As he lay in a nursing home unable to communicate in the traditional manner that most of us know, there was communication. These forms of communication came through dreams, gut feelings, the touching of his hands, tears that would roll down his cheek as she spoke to him, and the many hours of simply being present with one another.

Ten months after the accident, Barb had a pretty profound dream. There was a great deal of concern to whether Steve was able to visually see. He would open his eyes about a quarter of the way by pulling his eyebrows up which took great effort on his part. Barb truly felt that he was able to see when his eyes were even slightly open. All of the visual tests that the doctors performed were inconclusive and even though his family had hope, there was much doubt. One night after falling to sleep, she had a dream that Steve was partially conscious in his hospital bed. She handed an envelope and stamp that had a brightly colored peach on it (they had originally met in Georgia, the peach state). Her instructions, if he was able to see, were to place the stamp on the envelope. He did it correctly, although slightly crooked. The following day Barb went to visit Steve and she told him about the dream and that she knew he was able to see. She began using brightly colored objects to exercise his sight. As she moved an object back and forth in front of his eyes, she immediately noticed that one of his eyes began to follow it. After continuing this exercise, he was able to sync both eyes and follow an object whether it be a person or some other object. Barb relayed this to his family and they began conducting their own visual tests and realized that he did have the ability to see even though he lay in a comatose state. There were even times when a single tear would roll down his cheek; a tear of hope and love.

Barb would continue to visit Steve almost everyday for the duration of his short life. They would spend countless hours being present with one another. Even though only she was the only one doing the talking, there was definitely communication happening in her opinion. She always knew that he did understand her words and that he did see her and her astounding love for him. She refers to this time as a painfully joyous battle.

A final experience occurred that made it clear to Barb that the end of Steve's battle was near. " I was laying on my bed and this recognizable vibrational feeling consumed me and I was viewing my body from above. The spiritual part of me went and sat at the foot of my bed and stared into the mirror. My face was much older and worn and very tired looking. Then, my face changed and morphed into Steve's face. I couldn't tell if I was me or if I was him as both of our weathered faces were in my view. When I returned to my body, I knew that it was time to let go."

The next few visits that Barb made were spent assuring Steve that she would be okay if he was gone. She also confirmed to him that she realized how difficult this physical battle was for him. She urged him to let go so he could finally be at peace. Shortly after, he did pass and Barb was by his side when it happened. "With all of the grace that I could muster, I smiled at him and gave my gentle goodbye. After he took his final breath, I looked up at the ceiling. Even though I couldn't see anything, it was my confirmation to him that I knew where he was and where he was going."

That evening, Steve visited Barb in a dream. This was a much different kind of dream than the previous one. It was full of beautiful goodbyes.

Barb believes that all of her experiences nurtured the sensitivity that was needed to endure such a beautifully and tragic story. Her level of empathy has been heightened which causes her to be much more sensitive when it pertains to the negative aspects of her life. Her glimpse into the afterlife gave her profound insight into the beautiful "big picture." An insight that she considers to be the most valuable gift that has ever been bestowed upon her.

Your Own Elevated Life

The many amazing experiences that Barb has had happen to her throughout her life have been truly phenomenal. There is no concrete explanation for any of them although they did in fact occur. After learning of what had happened to her, I found myself wanting to find my own higher vibrational level. I wanted to have my own unique occurrences that could heighten my life. I hope that you had similar thoughts yourself after reading her story.

We all live our day to day lives and manage them the best we know how but how many of us really live with appreciation and a love for life? If you do then you should be very proud of yourself. I feel that the majority of the population does not do this. We tend to focus on what we don't have or what is wrong with us rather than focusing on what we do have and all of the incredible qualities we do possess. Most people that I have known or have come into contact with choose to live their lives either in survival mode or in a superficial "keeping up with the Joneses" mode. Both of these ways of living have little to no true happiness or fulfillment. Living your life in survival mode is nothing but stress and sadness. When living in this mindset, it can be extremely difficult to step back and pay attention to what makes us truly happy. The overwhelming stress of figuring out how to make it from one day to the next drowns us from soulful fulfillment. The latter way of living is, in my mind, the saddest way to live. Our society has created a superficiality that can lead to a very unhealthy lifestyle. Unfortunately, many people believe that material possessions and status will complete them and their life. Guess what? This could not be farther from the truth! Let the need for shallow stuff and social stature go and I promise you real contentment will come your way.

As human beings, we all have an inner vibration level that changes from moment to moment. The aspect of us that creates this vibration is our soul. The true essence of our soul vibrates at a very high level. There are many earthly and human circumstances that can lower this vibrational level. Negativity in general is the main contributor to this. I have come up with a couple analogies that resonate with me about this vibrational interruption. We have all fallen into a deep, peaceful, and dream-filled sleep many times in our lives. When in this deep sleep state, we are vibrating at a purely peaceful level. This is a wonderful state that I think we all appreciate very much. BAM!!!! The alarm goes off and our peace is interrupted and shattered. A brief death of a beautiful state of existence ensues. Yes, of course we need to wake up, but the abrasive sound of the alarm clock, in a sense, ruins a beautiful state.. The second analogy relates to a high level of vibration and may not be as common as the first. Have you met the love of your life? If you have then you can easily answer that question. If you have to think about it then I hope that you one day meet that special person. For those of you who have, you understand this vibrational analogy and hopefully your experience has not been interrupted and you will continue to experience this heightened form of vibrational earthly living. Unfortunately, mine was interrupted, disrupted, and completely destroyed. Even though this happened, I have found an equally heightened sense of living. I am grateful for all of my experiences whether they were negative or positive. They were all growth lessons that have benefited my life and my soul's growth.

Soul growth is an extremely important thing. It is actually the most important aspect of our existence. Without it, what would be the point? There would not be one! Within our short human lives we need to learn every possible lesson that is presented to us. Soak up the pain and struggle and turn it into an acceleration of growth that will benefit and project your soul further and further. Do not hide from difficulties and definitely do not bury the pain that you are feeling. Like I said, soak it up, learn from it, and benefit from it.

Elevation and Vibration are two words to always keep at the forefront of our lives. I also equate these words to Heighten and Connect. Each of our souls craves these things whether we consciously realize it or not. The best way to accomplish these concepts is to be present in every moment. Every second of our lives has so much knowledge to offer. It is up to us to be open to this knowledge and to learn from it. So many people don't take advantage of this offering and allow the lessons to pass them by. When we allow these lessons in, we then can connect or vibrate on a much higher level. Once we begin to live with a higher vibration, amazing things will begin to occur. Our ability to love and be loved will exceed our previous expectations. Also, our empathy and creativity will grow to a new level. When all of this begins to happen, our soul and the world we live in will do nothing but benefit. We, as individuals, need this and our world definitely needs this to happen.

Elevated vibration should be the goal of every human being. "Vibrating on high," as I will refer to it, is a way of being in tune with life and death as a whole. Our soul is vibrational purity, our physical being however is not. The soul doesn't have to work at its vibrational level, while when in our physical bodies, we definitely do have to work at this. This work is done through the practice of meditation, prayer, empathetic practices, creativity, and love.

We are all unique individuals. The main reason, in my opinion, that a good majority of people never find their own true path to happiness is their own fear and living under the control of others' fears. I recently found an amazing excerpt from the author Shanna Lee:

"We are taught to live within the ideals and resonance of those that raise us until we arrive at our teenage years where we either test the "rules" of life or cement them in their influence on us. If we decide to rebel against the ideals of others, we may spend the rest of our life pushing up against authority or we will begin to forge our own path. Sometimes that new path includes personal development work to rediscover our own soul frequency. Other times, while forging a different path, we stay disconnected from our own inner guidance.

If we never test the "rules" during our teenage years, we usually live within the dominant frequency of our surroundings for the remainder of our lives. The dominant frequency might feel similar enough to our own soul frequency that its resonance is comfortable; but for many, the dominant frequency is not in close resonance to their inner truth, which creates a life experience full of dissonance."

I believe that this couldn't be more accurate. We all need to be allowed to explore ourselves and the teenage years are when this begins to surface. If you are a parent as I am, encourage your children to find themself through whatever fulfills them. Try not to force them into the box that makes you happy and try not to mold or direct them through your own fears of the world. Foster their paths and you will raise very fulfilled children who will become fulfilled adults. Do you know what happens when the world is filled with adults that are truly fulfilled and happy? The world, as a whole, is fulfilled and happy!

Part Five
The Painter
Diego Walcopz

This chapter of the book is a little different from the others due to the fact that Diego does not speak English. Because of this, I was not able to conduct an interview with him. His account was translated by his wife and sent to me. When I read his story, I knew that I wanted to have it be part of the book. This is his experience told in the first person.

I was in bed and then suddenly I saw myself near the rooftop looking down at my body. I was floating and initially, I did not recognize that I was viewing my own body. I first asked myself, whose body could that be? It looked very strange to me in that moment. Finally I did recognize that it was mine. The next thing I knew, I heard a voice telling me, "come on." I felt that the voice I was hearing was near me, although I could not see an image of anyone. We began going up through a viaduct full of humid-like fog which was very refreshing. As we were traveling, I saw other viaducts with people going in an upwards direction just as we were. I thought to myself that I was leaving my life on the planet. I believed that my life had ended. I asked my guide if my life did end and the voice said, "it seems like it did."

As I left my body I experienced a sensation of an ascending pathway. I then flew to a place which was very calm and still. I noticed a subtle and bluish fog that was very dark and dim. I continued to ascend until I arrived in a place that seemed to be a small square.

There were two beings that stood before me. Although I knew they were there, I could only see their big eyes. I talked with them and asked them if I was leaving in a definite way and they answered, "maybe yes". I began to think to myself, "am I dreaming?" These guides told me that I was not dreaming and to look at my family. Standing in front of me were all of my family members who had previously passed away. There were also people that I did not know. Many of these individuals were children. They were all smiling and they were very happy to see me. When I tried to approach them, they told me not to. If I did, they would embrace me and I would feel such an indescribable love that it would be impossible for me to go back.

As I listened to their advice, an enormous prairie appeared before me. I noticed that there were many tunnels. At the bottom of these tunnels I was able to see people ascending to unknown places. Their heads looked very tiny as though they were far away even though they weren't. When they finally passed near me, they saluted me and said they were friends of someone that I knew. Others were totally unknown to me and it was ten years later that I met all of them for the first time on earth. They ended up being friends of my brother.

I continued to ascend and as I did, more and more beings communicated with me. I was told that my soul was in a vital transition and I was to talk with someone who would decide if I would come back to my body or not. They said that the more I ascended, there would be tremendous experiences and the possibility of coming back would diminish and I debated if I should go on or turn back.

In the blink of an eye, I was in a beautifully colored environment. The tonality of this place was that of a cream color with a shining red-orange accent. These intense colors behaved in an explosive manner. It was amazingly constant and very comforting. I entered a tube-like shape with a very bright bluish fog and I began traveling at a very high speed. The speed was so intense that I began to feel disoriented and somewhat lost. I was feeling very distanced from where I had begun my trip. In an instant, the intense speed slowed and I was able to see the two guides that had greeted me earlier.

The guides began a dialogue with me and a life review began. I relived many moments from my life and then I witnessed my entire life. As I viewed my life, a process of self-judgement began. I questioned decisions and choices that I had made throughout my life. I wondered what had caused me to make some of these choices. I began to become very inquisitive and I was seeking all of the answers to my own existence and the existence of the universe.

Suddenly, I viewed my inner self and noticed that I was in a conflict of understanding. I recognized that there was an overwhelming sense of fear (due to guilt) of overcoming and finally accepting all the occurrences and consciousness of each stage of my life. I began to understand the life that I had lived in its truest sense. There was no judgement from other beings that I encountered. There was however, my own extreme judgment of myself and the life I had led. My guides allowed me to understand all of the contradictions, actions, and situations in which I felt guilty throughout my life. Their words were precise and promoted my wellbeing and my inner peace. At one point when I was having a destructive dialogue with myself involving justification of my actions or placing the guilt on someone else, they simply said, everything that I was feeling was part of the game and part of my evolution. This evolution was one where everything we do is valid and important but our mistakes were excusable. Each of our earthly lives is a small puzzle piece that creates an enormous evolutionary puzzle.

I asked the guides if the life review that I was seeing could be slowed down so that I could talk about certain periods which I thought were important. They answered that they were not as important as I thought they were. I told them that I wanted to analyze each period lived however, they told me it was not necessary. All of their statements were said very kindly although I still felt frustrated. They told me not to worry about my self-analysis because there was no judgment at all. I then understood that I had to go on ascending.

I took a much needed rest in a quiet place, but at the same time kept ascending through a translucent tube. I looked at the people who were ascending with me and noticed that they were symbolically throwing away all of their earthly possessions as though they would not need them anymore. I also noticed in the distance, grayish beings that were being received by other beings who were helping them to leave their earth life. I knew that I needed to ascend further and I was to talk with a being and decide if I would return to my earthly life or not. I saw that some people were descending and returning to their lives and others were not.

I asked an individual that I seemed to know from my life on earth what he was doing there. He told me that he had a very serious health problem which caused his death, but the health problem had already been solved by the doctors. This is the reason why he was going back to his body. I then asked another individual, a friend of my family for many years, what he was doing. He told me that he was leaving the Earth realm in a definite way.

My guides approached me with a warm smile and took my hands in theirs. Our spirits traveled at great speed and there was a refreshing scent of cool menthol. I could hear high-pitched cosmic sounds that were similar to music and a beautiful white light. I felt an incredible wind within me; an internal breeze if you will.

Suddenly, we came to an abrupt stop. Standing in my pathway were many deceased members of my family and then a luminous, golden shape appeared; an androgynous being who was shining as bright as the sun but did not hurt my eyes. This being grew in size as it approached me until it became a little bigger than me. I felt marveled at the greatest beauty I had ever seen. This being overflowed with compassion, love, and all-knowingness. I looked at the being face to face and it occurred to me that if I chose to view it's real shape, it would be equivalent to staying. The being surrounded me with an embrace that was tender and noble. I understood all aspects of the universe and thanked the being for allowing me to decide my fate and for allowing me to have this marvelous experience. He extended his hand to me and I took it onto mine. The being slowly lowered down his hand and with deep understanding went away.

I told my guides that I humbly was thankful for them and for allowing me to have such an amazing experience. In a soft voice, I told them that I still had some things to do on earth. They told me my life would continue to be just as tortuous as it had always been. There would be some accomplishments and it would last for the time that it was planned to last. My earthly life had been carefully planned before my incarnation. I accepted what they had told me.

I was not fearful to return to my earthly life. Once the decision was made for me to return, we started to ascend at great speed without friction and without effort. I found it difficult to withstand the friction and the unbearable noise. When I could not bear it anymore, the guides told me to hold on. The guides told me to relax because I would soon arrive. Suddenly, I saw myself hovering above my body. A being then appeared and told me I had to go into the body. I finally fell into my body. I was on the bed with my eyes open and burning. I felt a deep pain near my heart that was almost unbearable. I was having great difficulty breathing. I was rigid and my arms could not move. My feet were frozen and I could not move them either. I could only allow small threads of air to enter my lungs.

I fell into a deep sleep for the next twelve hours. When I woke up, I remembered how the guides told me how my wife, my daughter, and I would die. I saw all of our complete futures. I was told that I would only remember fragments of my experience and only during certain moments of my life. I also remembered the guides telling me that my life would continue as tortuous as it had been, but with small accomplishments. These struggles were a crucial way to experience things and to learn and grow as a soul.

The Painted Growth of your Life

Diego's experience changed him in many ways. He learned to become more adaptable to difficult circumstances and began to understand the evolution of the soul. He was witness to his past, future, and death although he would remember very little. Even though his physical memory could not retain all that he experienced, his soul's memory would always remember everything. He was told by his guides that this lack of remembering was crucial for him to continue on his earthly journey. This crucial piece of information pertains to all of our lives and memories. Our veil must remain down so that we are able to focus on this life and not our past experiences. Mental memories can, at times, hinder and get in the way of our growth. They can sometimes slow us down and create growth obstacles. Although many of our memories are extremely comforting and joyous, they do not always aide in our future. Some individuals get stuck in the past which slows our growth as a soul. Learn from your past, but do not live within its restraints.

Diego now knows that we are all predestined cosmic particles placed upon a path of growth and learning. We are always free to grow in our own consciousness with the use of our own individual free will. Regardless of how predetermined our path is on earth, the soul is free to learn or not to learn the lessons that are presented. Our evolution is one of wisdom, forgiveness, and love. We will not be judged in any way for we only judge ourselves which then leads to the greatest growth. Never fear the message of some individuals and of some faiths that teach that at the end you will be judged and condemned for the life that you have led and the decisions that you have made. Sin does not exist in my opinion. Also, do not avoid your own individual judgement of yourself as your life progresses. Just remember to always keep in mind that none of us are perfect and we each make our own mistakes. Honestly, without mistakes, what would be the point of this roller coaster of a journey? Embrace each and every one of your mistakes. Allow them to teach you and to humble you. It's funny that, at least from my point of view, when someone admits they made a mistake we admire them yet we feel embarrassed or ashamed of ourselves when we make a mistake. The next time you find yourself amidst your own error, stop and tell everyone around you, "I just screwed up!" You will be amazed how good it actually makes you feel.

Think of your life as a painting. I know this is a difficult concept to imagine but just try. When each one of us sits down to paint our life's story, what will be the approach? Well, that varies from person to person and soul to soul (the soul is the actual executive producer overseeing the accumulation of our complete story). Some may paint an extremely detailed and honest portrait while others paint a big beautiful house with many expensive cars in the driveway. Some will paint in dollar signs while others will paint using a palette of love and creativity. How will you paint yours? I deeply hope that you paint using truth and sincerity. If you do this, your canvas will be so much brighter and full of beautiful textural strokes. It will be filled with beauty and realization of what really matters in this life. The "stuff" comes and goes and holds no significance. The love, empathy, and creativity are the colors that stand the test of time. They are the brightest of colors, vibrant and miraculous. They are the colors that make the world a better place and make all of us better human beings and souls.

Interlude

Pause,
Reflect,
Be,
Know what is ahead

Where we have been is very important. Where we are is also very important but where we are headed at the end of our physical life is crucial. It is crucial for one simple reason: that reason is that there is absolutely no finality to you or me; there is only progression. Imagine an infinite trail through the woods. The trail never ends. We walk along the trail finding new discoveries and we learn all about the trail and everything that inhabits it. We learn and learn until we eventually collapse from exhaustion. Although we collapse, only our physicality collapses, not our true self. Our true self never collapses; our true self is our soul. The soul is only pure and positive energy which can never collapse.

Relish each day that you are given and live it completely. Have appreciation for the path that you are allowed to walk upon and to explore. Fulfill your dreams and your desires and do not allow anything or anyone to stifle them. DO EVERYTHING THAT MSKES YOU HAPPY! Pardon my language but, FUCK ANYONE THAT ATTEMPTS TO TELL YOU OTHERWISE! Live your life with no regrets.

A regret is a hindrance that can trip up your happiness. Do not trip and stumble upon regrets throughout your life. Lead your life with purpose but just make sure that it is a true purpose and not a superficial one or one that is the purpose of someone else. Be who you are. Submerge yourself in love and creativity and be completely empathetic and always walk in the other person's shoes. After all, those shoes could be yours someday. Know your own path but at the same time always understand the path of the individual who is standing in front of you.

Just always keep these two thoughts in the back of your head:

1. Lay upon your death bed with not a single regret

2. At the end of your physical days you will be given a freeness that will engulf you and truly release your soul into pure bliss.

If you live your life knowing these two truths, you will live fulfilled.

Part Six
Morgana
Her Walk Towards the Truth

The following story is one that has a uniqueness all its own. When thinking about the stories I wanted to use for this book, I really wanted to have various types of stories. I know that there are so many varieties of NDE stories that have occurred throughout time and one of my main reasons for choosing different types was to allow individuals to tell their own. Someone may not feel comfortable talking about their story because they have convinced themself that it wasn't real or it was a hallucination of sorts. Maybe, just maybe they will stumble upon this book and read one of the chapters and think, "that's similar to what happened to me. Maybe it was real and maybe I should share it with the world." Please share your experiences. I guarantee it will only help you and this world of ours. That was one of my goals when setting out to write this book.

I would also like to add that this story is not only an amazing one but it touched me a little more personally due to the fact that I've had the extreme pleasure of knowing and being friends with this person for many, many years.

Morgana is an individual who has endured many struggles throughout her life. Previous events such as death, loss of love, loss of a job, loss of relationships, loss of family and friends, betrayal, and at times, loss of self provided many life lessons. She always has found a way to dive deep within herself to bounce back and become a stronger person while always knowing that difficulties and pain equal growth. Even though she has had so many of these life lessons, Morgana had no idea that 2020 would be one of the most pivotal and life changing years of her life.

The new year started like any other with months passing with the normal routine of work, activities, spending time with friends and family, serving and volunteering in the community, enjoying the outdoors and simply living in the moment. As the summer arrived with great anticipation, Morgana was looking forward to spending time in the mountains hiking and camping. This anticipation was abruptly halted when she received a phone call that abnormalities were found in her mother's bloodwork. Initially there was little concern as this was something they had become accustomed to throughout her mother's health journey and having always worked in the medical field, she knew the initial answer was simple because the lab work would be redrawn and she would then follow up with her doctor. Unfortunately, despite having overcome many similar abnormal lab values in the past, which were usually treated easily with a change in medication or an occasional blood transfusion, this would not be the case. Living several states away from her mother, Morgana began to make arrangements to travel home to be by her mother's side during the additional testing that would take place. Being a seasoned registered nurse, she was not overly concerned and had complete confidence that her mother would overcome whatever it was that was causing these abnormalities. Despite this confidence, there would be a diagnosis that either of them could have ever prepared for. At seventy-four years of age she was diagnosed with advanced B-Cell Leukemia. As treatment began, there were high hopes and due to the fact that she had been asymptomatic, the strong possibility of a full recovery was in everyone's mind. Although this was the case, she took a turn for the worse and within six weeks she was gone. Morgana had lost not only her mother but also her best friend. It was beyond devastating and there were no words to express the void that was felt with this loss.

Following the passing of her beloved mother, the months of July through November continued on with moments of adjusting to her loss and attempting to get back to as close to a version of normal life that was possible. Days were filled with the tasks of managing the final affairs of her estate, adjusting to having lost both her best friend and mom in one fell swoop, getting back to work, and trying to find a way to transition back to living life.

As the holiday season approached, many emotions were felt. Realizing that this would be the first season of holidays without her mother, Morgana felt an inner need and importance to surround herself with family and friends while also focusing on her mother's memory and how she always made that time of year very special.

Thanksgiving arrived and it was a day filled with many fond memories of her mom and appreciation for the time that they had shared together prior to her untimely death. Morgana also allowed herself to reflect on all of the areas of her life that she was truly blessed with. She had a home, family, friends, career, education, and her health to be thankful for. The holiday was celebrated in the traditional style like that of most of her previous Thanksgivings. As she enjoyed the day, she had no idea of the events that would follow that would forever change that evening and her life forever.

As dinner came to a close with family and friends, they said their goodbyes and Morgana began her journey home. It was a cool evening and traffic on I-25, a major highway in Colorado, was very heavy. She was tired and made the decision not to take the usual route home but to take the backroads thinking it would be much faster. The sky had turned dark as she travelled on these much less crowded roads; roads that she had driven many times over the past eighteen years of living in Colorado. She was relaxed and feeling at ease until car trouble ensued. Her initial thought was how could this be happening when she prided herself in the excellent care that she took in the condition of her vehicle. As Morgana pulled to the side of the dark road, she noticed that her cell phone had died and she had no way of charging it and therefore no way to contact anyone for help. As she sat in her car patiently waiting for someone to drive by, the temperature began dropping and the cold and dark night was engulfing her. Adding to the coldness was her attire. She was wearing holiday attire and holiday shoes, not the type of clothing that would be helpful in this situation. Weighing her options of waiting for help to come or beginning the four mile journey on foot, she decided on the latter. She rationalized with herself that because she was an avid hiker and was in relatively good shape, this choice would not be overly difficult and would get her home in a relatively short amount of time. It was around nine o'clock pm and she figured to be home no later than ten-thirty.

I do not remember much about my walk home, although deep down, I felt as though I was floating and surrounded by a light as I walked. Also, I do not have any recollection of the route that I took, however I do remember the floating and light feeling that I felt. It was almost as though my soul was free and I was viewing myself from above. I could not feel the ground beneath my feet or any part of my body. I logically knew that I was watching my body move but I had no participation in the physical act of moving. I could see all of the details of my surroundings, my clothing, hair, and my body's movements. Watching from above, I had a sense of needing to help guide my body home as I realized that the route I was taking was not the way that I should have been going. Initially, I was very worried about the direction I was taking but that worry quickly diminished with the realization that my being present from above could guide me home, which it did.

As I approached my house, I was still above my physical body and I helped to guide my hands to the keypad on the garage. As I was watching from above, I could see my hands fumble to enter the code to open the garage door. I also noticed my facial expression of not being able to remember the code. I glanced at the grass in front of me and noticed that frost had started to accumulate on the blades and I remember thinking how odd that was. After all, it was surely only eleven-o'clock pm at the latest.

As the journey progressed, my presence from above continued. I began to enter back into my body to see if I could help remember the garage door code but I could not. At that moment, I turned to my right and witnessed bright, yet soft figures approaching me. These beings emanated tremendous warmth. I could not make out their faces but was drawn to the fact that I knew they were definitely there to assist me in the darkness. As they moved closer, one of the figures wrapped their arms around me while the other helped to guide my hand to enter the garage door code. At that moment the faces revealed themselves to me. The figure helping me with the code was Jesus while the other was that of my mom. She was wrapping herself around me. This realization not only was aiding me in getting out of this horrific situation, it also left me in great awe. As I moved into the house, they both vanished and again I was witnessing the situation from above. I watched as my body moved towards the bathroom and drew a warm bath.

The bathroom had only a nightlight lit and as I sat on the side of the tub and began to remove my shoes, I noticed a dark liquid flowing onto the floor. It was dripping quite rapidly from what appeared to be my feet. Continuing to watch from above, I helped to guide my body over to the light switch to get a better assessment of my apparent injury. The blood was flowing heavily from areas on the bottoms of my feet where the skin was gone. Also, I noticed several parts that had turned purplish black in color. I knew from my many years of emergency-room nursing that this was not a good thing and that I had sustained frostbite. It was also at this point, as my body began to warm, that I began to experience the worst physical pain that I had ever endured. Somehow I found the strength to bandage my wounds the best I could and call for medical assistance. I also came to the realization that it was four-o'clock in the morning. That meant that I had been walking in the bitter cold for over seven hours with no recollection of the majority of my journey home. The only definite memory I had was that of making it to the field and to the garage door.

When I arrived to the emergency room, the diagnosis of frostbite was confirmed and they admitted me for immediate treatment. A second, and excruciating, journey was about to begin for me. The next couple of months were filled with a wide range of new feelings. Being in the burn unit, I was forced to endure painful dressing changes and multiple surgeries involving skin grafts to both feet. While being forced to experience the worst pain of my life, I was also facing possible amputation. Nothing could calm the pain or the constant replaying of the events that occurred on that long Thanksgiving walk home. There was so much of that night that I had no recollection of, however the moments that I could recall were beyond comforting. All I was able to do was lay in that hospital bed and ponder what my fate would be. It dawned on me that just as I could not save my mom from her fate, I could not save mine either."

Morgana's recovery was lengthy and difficult. She was unable to walk and was forced to rely on crawling until the skin grafts could heal. As the healing began, she had to relearn how to walk. Not knowing if the pain would forever be a part of her life and having to rely on others to help her with the daily tasks of bathing, cooking, cleaning, and dressing, she continued to forge forward. Also the lingering possibility of amputation had not been ruled out.

She was scheduled for one final surgery that could possibly end in amputation. "As I entered the surgery on that January morning, I knew that those next couple of hours could change my life forever. I closed my eyes and reflected upon the images of my mom and Jesus from my journey. I prayed and asked for guidance that I would make it through the surgery and that the amputation would not be necessary." As the medical team got her settled into the operating room and the anesthesiologist asked that she count backwards from ten, a familiar experience occurred. Just as during her walk through the cold darkness that night many months earlier, she exited her body to hover above and protect.

Waking from the surgery, Morgana looked down anxiously to know what her future would hold. She could see the numerous bandages that covered both of her feet. The amount of bandages were excessive, which in her mind, could only mean one thing, her feet were gone. Tears began to flood her eyes and the fear set in. A short time later, the surgeon and a nurse entered the room to discuss the details of the surgery. They expressed how they were completely shocked that the tissue on the area of her wounds had experienced a deeper level of healing on their own and the amputation was not needed.

The experiences that took place during November 2020 to January 2021 changed Morgana's life in ways that she never thought possible. She no longer had fear of anything, including death. She now cherishes life as well as the journey that follows our earthly lives. She firmly knows and believes that there is a heavenly afterlife and that her faith in God is real and that our loved ones who have passed will be awaiting us when we pass over. Another take away from the experience was that pain is a blessing as it allows for a deeper feeling of self-awareness and realization that our soul is very special and unique. Although this was truly one of the most difficult experiences of her life, she sums it up in one beautiful declaration. "I will forever be thankful for my Thanksgiving journey for it has made my life so much more complete."

How can we walk towards our own truth?

All of our lives begin basically in the same manner. We are conceived, fostered within the womb, and born. Once born, our physical journey begins. Think of your life like that of Dorothy in The Wizard of Oz. It is a walk that you take brick by brick until that last step is taken at the end of your life and the curtain is pulled down to reveal true happiness and truth. Each brick is a moment or an experience that is crucial to your own growth. We can choose to run as fast as we can, not paying much attention to each brick, or we can make it a point to look at the details of each brick. We can miss it all or we can pay attention and take it all in and savor the details. Each and every detail, whether it be a second, minute, day, or a year, is astonishing in its own right. Have you ever heard someone say, "I'm just wasting time until…..?" We purposefully waste time until whatever it is will occur. So many of these moments are tossed away beneath the viewpoint of being unimportant or unimpressive. We spend so much of our time waiting for that next amazing moment when the moment right in front of us is amazing; next time just take a closer look at it. You will begin to see it and revel in it. These important details are the building blocks of our earthly lives which add up to to the ultimate accumulation of our soul's life. Your soul wants you to pay attention to the details.

When we venture out on a long walk, many aspects often occur. Sometimes there is great joy but often there can also be pain. Aches in your joints and muscles can definitely slow the journey while the warm sun on our back and the smells of nature can create happiness. The sun on our back…this is responsible for inspiring our happiest moments. That sun, light, and warmth that moves us and energizes us to move from moment to moment and from day to day is so crucial. Although the sun's warmth sparks our growth, so do those aches I was speaking of. We all experience the aches of life. The aches are just as important as the warmth of the sun. These aches allow the warmth to stand out and be noticed. Always remember that without pain, there is no pleasure. We need both to create a balance and appreciation for our existence.

Once our physical life comes to an end, our soul continues on. Our soul's walk never ends. The sun is always shining upon its back and always guiding the way. The soul may shed its shell but it never expires. The soul never runs out of bricks on its infinite journey. It continues to accumulate its own stack of bricks from life to life. We need to take a step back from our physical lives and realize that we are so much more than what we see day to day. We are not our morning routine or our occupation. We are not our yearly vacations or our social desires. We are a soul. A soul that seeks nothing but the truth. The truth that we all know deep down at our core. The truth that exceeds the Mercedes in the garage and the square footage of our home. Your soul, my soul, and the neighbor down the street's soul are all that matters.

Morgana's walk was an extremely painful experience while being the most enlightening one of her life thus far. The physical pain that she endured is unimaginable for the majority of us. The realization that emerged from this pain is something that she would not trade for the world. Pain is something that none of us want though it is the one thing that creates the greatest growth in our lives. Whether that pain is physical, mental, or emotional, it forces us to be stronger and it also helps us to appreciate the non-painful times. My favorite mantra is "lean into the sharp points." I have recently added a second part to this saying. "Lean into the sharp points and cherish the soft points." Even my ten year old daughter gets this aspect of life. The other day we were talking about a difficult and painful experience that she experienced a few years ago. Her exact words were, "that experience made me stronger and more able to deal with difficult situations." I couldn't have said it better myself. That sums up life for all of us. So do not be frightened by life's pain and struggle because it will benefit you whether you realize it or not.

Morgana's walk towards her own truth is an extreme version of everyone's walk. Her strength and faith were solidified with each and every step that she took on that cold and dark night. Her soul now knows the truth of this life and the truth of what comes next after this life. Just as her walk enhanced her own existence and viewpoint, allow your own walk to be enhanced with each and every step that you take. Never ever forget to look down at your bricks. After all, they are yours and yours alone. Do not let any of those bricks go unnoticed!

Part Seven
The Carpenter King
Scott Kurrle

Up to this point I have been referring to each of these experiences as stories. This all changed on a Sunday morning in early December. I had read a brief NDE "story" from a man who lives in Georgia that intrigued me. I sent him a message and asked if he would be interested in an interview and possibly using his "story" for this book. He was interested and we set a time to talk.

Over the past year, I have been conducting many interviews and each one has taught me something new. Initially I attempted to structure the discussions with specific questions but as I conducted more and more interviews, I quickly learned to just sit back and listen and let the agenda go; just listen and let these amazing people talk. Scott Kurrle was one of these amazing people I was privileged to be able to listen to.

"This isn't my story, this is my testimony," he explained to me. This is how Scott referred to his experiences and it really resonated with me. He was absolutely correct. This is his testimony, not just a story. Keep in mind the word ineffable as you are reading his testimony. So many of these experiences are so difficult to explain using our human language.

It is difficult to explain an unearthly and non-physical occurrence with the earthly words we have access to.

Scott Kurrle is a man whom I spoke to on December fifth of 2021. I had read some of his story previously and was very interested in finding out more about his life and his NDE experiences. Yes, you read that last sentence correctly, he used the word experiences, as in plural. As we spoke for over two hours that Sunday morning, I could hear the sincerity in his words. He was full of life and there seemed to be a sense of urgency within him to share what he had experienced with me and with the world. He was the first person I had spoken to who had numerous NDE occurrences where he had actually been deceased twice. His life was unlike any I had ever met or spoken to.

Scott King was born to an Italian mother and American Navy father. At the age of seven, his father left and his mother became homeless. Scott was placed in foster care and was eventually adopted at the age of twelve and became Scott Kurrle. His adoptive parents, a school teacher and an attorney, had the means to live a very comfortable life which was a far stretch from the life he had previously known.

Scott was fifteen years old when his first NDE experience occurred. His parents had decided to take a lengthy vacation although they sent Scott to stay with his grandparents on their farm. It was a working farm and Scott did enjoy helping out his uncle with the day to day chores. One day he and his uncle were out in the field spraying the potatoes with pesticides to keep the bugs from getting to them. His uncle was driving an old 1950's tractor while Scott maneuvered the tank sprayer on the trailer to the rear of the tractor while also making sure that the sprayer didn't clog. While standing on the bar of the trailer, his shoe string became caught between the fender and the rear tire of the tractor. The shear force of the tractor pulled Scott under the massive tire. He attempted to yell for his uncle to stop but the engine was far too loud and his cries for help went unnoticed. He began to feel his ankle and foot being crushed and his back being separated as though his torso was being torn into two sections. His entire body was being thrashed between the wheel and the fender of the old tractor. Scott's skull was beginning to suffer the crushing trauma of force and the next thing that happened was pure blackness. He lost consciousness for a period of time and when he gained consciousness, his pain was gone and he was at peace.

The tranquility began to set in as Scott left his physical body and began to float above the tractor where his uncle was still unaware that anything wrong had happened. He was witnessing the potato plants and the farmland below him. He described what he was witnessing with great wonderment. "Everything was so amazingly beautiful. It was as though I was seeing it all with angel eyes." As he continued to float alongside the tractor, he wondered if this was heaven. It had to be heaven he thought. Everything he was witnessing had a WOW factor to it. The potato plants, the air, the land…the only word he could use to describe it all was, WOW. He was witnessing the pure beauty of it all.

All the while Scott was floating, he sensed a voice whisper something into the left ear of his uncle. "Kevin," the voice simple stated. Who's voice was this? Who was trying to send a message to his uncle? Whoever it was, the message was heard loud and clear. Uncle Kevin heard the message and silenced the tractor. He proceeded to get down off of the tractor and walk along the side of the it and the sprayer that was attached. Strangely, there was no sight of his nephew. As he took a closer look, he saw the unimaginable; Scott's twisted and crushed body was in his view. All he could say was, "Oh my God, Oh my god!"

As Scott was viewing all of this from above, he wanted to communicate to his uncle that he was ok. No matter how much he tried and what means he took, his uncle could not hear him. He shouted and shouted in a empty attempt to communicate with no success. He even attempted to stand in front of him but this failed as his uncle passed right through him. Kevin rushed to get his truck to transport Scott to the hospital. He witnessed his his body being placed into the truck.

As I listened to Scott tell this part of his experience, something blatantly stood out to me. He never said, "my body." He never referred to viewing "his body." Every time, he used the words, "the body." I really found this fascinating. I didn't stop him to ask why he chose to use these select words because I just knew. He knew that the body was just a shell and it wasn't truly him.

As his uncle left the farm with "the body," Scott stayed right along side of him. They arrived at the hospital and the medical staff began to assess the situation. Scott noticed as he moved throughout the hospital, he effortlessly passed through walls and barriers. No one in the hospital noticed him; he was physically invisible. He was witness to his uncle vigorously explaining to the doctors and staff what had happened to his nephew.

In an instant, Scott found himself underneath the stretcher where his physical body lay. They entered a room where the medical staff attempted to resuscitate the body. Scott watched from above as cpr was preformed along with defibrillator shocks to the heart. Even though all of this was shocking to witness, Scott still only had the feeling of, WOW. Everything was WOW to him. As he continued to use this word in my interview with him, it gave me the feeling of when a young child is in awe of everything that is new to them. This made me think of how children are pure just as the human soul is only made of complete purity.

The next thing that occurred was astonishing and medically unexplainable. Scott saw a large flash from an old-time camera and he was instantly back in his body. He felt himself attempt to take a breath and his heart begin to beat again. He had been dead for somewhere between an hour and a half to two hours. Everyone was astonished and in disbelief.

As Scott gained consciousness and his eyes began to see again, he saw his grandparents in the room with him. The doctors explained to him how badly injured his leg was and that he may have to endure an amputation. As he heard the news, he wanted to speak but was unable to due to the fact that his jaw had been badly broken. The doctors continued to explain that if they didn't remove his leg, he could die from the severe infection. Although this medical diagnosis was given, another miracle happened; his leg began to heal and no amputation was necessary.

He was eventually released from the hospital and returned to his grandparent's home to continue to recover. Even though the amputation wasn't necessary, Scott was practically paralyzed from the accident. He had lost all hope and wanted to die (again) but as the days and weeks went by, he began to regain feeling in his lower extremities and was able to return to life as he once had known.

Scott returned to school although he had a difficult time focusing and had to learn how to write again. After high school, he made the decision to enter the military as a marine. When the medical evaluation was conducted upon entering, his past injuries were somehow not identified and he was able to enter boot camp. He was ecstatic that his injuries had not hindered his goal of a military acceptance. One day while on a run, Scott collapsed. He was medically re-evaluated and discharged from the marines. Even though he was devastated by the discharge, something positive came from it. Part of his re-evaluation was a lie detector exam. He thought to himself, "the truth about my experience will finally come out." He passed the exam with flying colors although skepticism was still apparent amongst those who conducted the lie detector test. This validation, even though not believed by others, solidified to Scott that his experience did indeed happen.

Scott, once again, settled back into daily life. He began working as a carpenter building houses and working for a lumber company. At the age of twenty-eight he made a move to Gainesville, Florida and had taken on a side job as a security guard. He was asked by a friend if he would help with security for his daughter's sweet sixteen party. The party was to be out in the country practically in the middle of nowhere and he didn't want any strangers stumbling upon the party and causing a disruption. Scott gladly agreed to help out.

As he made his way through the countryside, he had difficulty finding the property where the party was to be held. There were no street signs which made this a difficult task. He eventually found the party and made his way in. Being there early, he noticed a huge brush pile that would make for a bonfire for the party. His friend was pouring gasoline from the pile to create an ignition trail to light the pile. He asked Scott to light it for him. In an instant there was an enormous explosion and Scott was lifted into the air. He realized that his body was on fire and he was burning everywhere. His hair had been completely burned off and he was in extreme pain. As he breathed in the flames, he thought to himself, "I need to run and put myself out." He eventually was able to get away from the bonfire, roll on the ground, and extinguish the flames. The girlfriend of his friend was a nurse and knew she needed to get him into cold water to lower his body temperature. They quickly filled the bathtub with cold water and ice. As he lay in the cold water with steam rising into the air, his skin was blistering and falling off of his body. He began to go into shock and thought, "God is finally taking me back to heaven for good."

For the second time in his life, Scott left his physical body and the pain and anguish he was experiencing from the horrific accident was gone just as with the tractor accident. He felt himself exiting the house through the ceiling and floating over the trees. He continued up and up and he felt an incredible sense of peace. "I want to finally be away from this world that has been so painful," he thought to himself.

As the peace overtook him, he heard a voice which evolved into a choir of voices. The higher he floated, the volume of the voices lowered. In a glorious instant he heard a female voice say, "I Love You." Scott was curious who was communicating this to him. All he could feel was extreme warmth and was worried that it would end and he would once again be sent back to the pain of his body. "You're not sending me back." As he had this thought, he felt as if he was in a slingshot and was catapulted away from everything and into an even greater feeling of peace. For some reason, and even though he did not want to return to his body, he wanted to see his physical body but was unable to accomplish this. Scott found himself in complete darkness and all of his thoughts began to fade away. Off into the darkness, he saw what appeared to be a star. He interpreted this to be a tunnel of sorts. "This is the tunnel that everyone talks about when they exit the physical world and travel to the spiritual world." The single star became a wall of stars and he found himself within this infinite amount of stars. He thought, "I don't need food, water, air or anything. I absolutely need nothing."

A separate star off in the distance was moving closer and closer to him at an incredible speed. It occurred to Scott that this star was to be his next life. He felt two hands grip him under his arms. He felt the hands begin to tickle him which made him giggle and just like that, he transformed from that of an adult to a child and eventually to an infant. This infant form of Scott fell into a deep slumber. He exited this slumber as a ghost. A ghost who had the ability to lay down into a body in heaven.

The next thought that Scott had was, "where are all of the angels?" While having this thought, he could see two hallways appearing before him. One hallway was pure light while the other was filled with pure darkness. He noticed three individuals, his friend who had asked him to start the bonfire, the friend's girlfriend who had helped him into the cold bath, and a nurse. They all appeared to be very unhappy. He did not want to go towards them and wanted to avoid their unhappiness. He decided to travel into a different direction where he saw a desk, kitchen, living room and many more people. Scott heard one of these people say to him, "you are a ghost, get away." The next thing he knew, he found himself at a dark doorway. Although it was very dark, he could see the light of the porch at the front of his friend's house. His friend approached him and said, "dude, you were dead for a really long time. What was heaven like?" Scott found himself back in his body, again. He could hear his friend's girlfriend shouting to get him to the hospital. Scott had been dead for nearly four hours; much longer than the first time he had been deceased.

As he arrived at the hospital, just as when he was fifteen, he was assessed by the medical staff and a plan to save him was put into effect. Scott's body was very badly burned and the doctors believed skin grafts were necessary to save him but Scott did not agree. He wanted his wounds to heal naturally. He was somehow lucid enough to leave the hospital on his own free will. He was determined to recover from his burns at home and on his own terms. For the next year, he treated his burns with natural remedies. Remarkably, Scott does not have any scars from the terrible burns.

Like I said at the beginning of this chapter, Scott's life and testimony was unlike any other I had encountered. He is an amazing and resilient person and his experiences are incredible and definitely ineffable.

You Are the King of Your Own Castle

What does it mean to be a king? Obviously we all know what the historical and royal meaning is but there are so many other ways to define this title. Simply put, a king is a ruler. Now this usually entails the ruling of many individuals, however it does not have to only be regarded in this way. What if we were each able to view ourselves as the king of our own self and our of our own existence? Sounds pretty good huh?

So many people feel as if they have no choices when it pertains to their lives. We all have choices, we just have to find the courage deep down within us to make those choices. Steer away from the "black and white" teachings of our society and find your gray area of true happiness. The things in life that truly make our soul happy are found in the gray areas of life. The "black and white" are in my opinion, where the bullshit lies. We are taught from day one to live within certain parameters and to also succeed within those same parameters. If we live by our soul's desires, we will stray from what society tells us we should equate to. Sometimes, straying is the correct path. Our life's sum or answer should be based on what makes us happy. Happiness, as a theme, has been subjected to what society deems to be true. How can a mass of individuals tell you what will make you happy? They do not know you and what pleases you so why do we listen to what we are being told? After all, society's norms are nothing but a mass of fear. A fear to be judged and left out of the party. Remember being a kid and hoping that the popular kids would ask you to play with them at recess or invite you to the party? We all do. As a kid, I get this need for this acceptance but as an adult, I have never understood this. What makes me happy, does not make you happy and vice versa. Society should have no say in our choices that will determine our future. This is where we can go back to what it is to be our own king. Who makes a king's choices? The king does.

Our path is ours and no one else's. Deep down, we all know this yet we conform to the path that others lay in front of us. Why is it that we do this? Is it merely for acceptance from those around us or could it be that we have a deep-seeded fear that our own path choice will fail us? My guess is that it is a combination of the two. All of this circles back to our gut. Like I have stated so frequently, that feeling or knowing that we all have is our gut which in turn is our soul quietly screaming at us to listen to it. The problem is that our brain steps in and overrides our soul. The human brain tends to immediately find flaws and skepticism in our truth. Yes, our brain serves as a protective shield within our lives and we need it for millions of other tasks but we need to learn when it is serving us positively and when it is serving us in a negative way. The soul and the brain can coincide with one another to create a prosperous future for us all just as spiritually and science are capable of the same. The Yin and Yang, which creates lively balance, are the brain and soul if you will. The gray areas of our lives tend to weave their paths in between the black and white of our Yin and Yang.

There is another task that the brain tends to focus upon in great deal for many people…"why me?" This question can pertain to many aspects of life. Why is my life so difficult? Why can't I have a life like so and so? Why was I born? While speaking with Scott about his experiences, he would frequently ask, "why did I survive and others didn't?" This is a difficult question to live with and attempt to find an answer to. The advice that I gave was simply, those questions do not require concrete answers. Life is whatever it is supposed to be whether that means dying at a young age, living to one-hundred, struggling through constant hardships, or living a life of luxury. We each are learning the lessons that our soul is in search of. The next time you have a tough experience, try to take a minute and tell yourself that. Your soul will appreciate it and your brain will enjoy the needed rest.

If you have read this far then I assume you are, for the most part, on board with what this book has had to say. If this is the case, I would like to present a challenge to you. If you are unhappy with the way your life has played out thus far, sit down and ask yourself a question: what would make me happy? What is it that you always had an interest in but maybe never pursued? What excites you? Maybe it is some form of art or possibly learning an instrument. Could it be to start your own business or to travel the works? It could be so many endless possibilities just waiting for you to reach down inside and say, I am going to do what makes me happy. If you are stuck in a cubicle day in and day out and you despise it, then change it. Don't wait for the next thirty years to pass you by. Don't live a life of misery. Make those future years something that is amazing and fulfilling. You possess the ability to get the hell away from the black and white world you were taught and live for the gray happiness that is awaiting you. All you have to do is make the decision to do it.

MAKE THAT DECISION

MAKE YOUR OWN HAPPINESS

My Past with "I"

Eight hours ago this chapter did not exist. Seven hours ago it did. I'm sure that makes no sense to you at all, but it will. As I stated previously, I have never had an NDE. Something else that I had never done was a past life regression. I had read about them but I never really thought about participating in one until a friend of mine told me about her aunt who was a hypnotherapist and past life regressionist. She talked with me about her experiences with her aunt and I was instantly intrigued and knew that I had to experience this for myself.

I contacted Denise Fedelleck to discuss her process when it pertained to last life regression. I could instantly tell that she was an extremely kind person and I instantly felt comfortable speaking with her. We spoke for quite a while and chose a day that would work for both of us. A Friday in early January would be the day.

I arrived to her home, which was somewhat remote and had a beautiful view of the Rocky Mountains, in the late morning on that Friday. We sat in her living room discussing her background and how the process would proceed. I was beyond excited for this experience, although I had a little concern that I wouldn't be able to be hypnotized. I had witnessed people being hypnotized and they appeared to be completely controlled by the hypnotist and without any free will of their own. Although I was wondering if I would be able to do this, I entered into this with absolutely no expectations; I was just going to go with it and whatever happened would happen.

She took me into the room where we would proceed. I settled into the comfortable reclining chair that would hold me for the next two hours. As my eyes closed and the serene sound of Denise's voice guided me to explore my soul's past, I was excitedly prepared for what was about to show itself to me. We started with some relaxing words and deep breathing. The main key to this experience is to focus on your breath and to make your mind a clean slate. Extinguishing thoughts throughout all of of this is, in my opinion, the most difficult part. The human brain is constantly firing thought after thought and to silence these is quite a challenge. I pictured an open window and whenever a thought or worry would enter, I would simply usher it out the window. This exercise proved to work. It did not stop the thoughts but it did force them to leave my mind.

I was relaxed and ready to proceed. Denise had me envision a staircase. Mine was one that lead to a basement, which I liked since I have always loved basements ever since I was a kid (probably all of the tornado preparation as a kid growing up in Nebraska). I slowly, one stair at a time, walked down the staircase. By this time, I was extremely relaxed, however I maintained where my physical body was. I did not lose my actual and present existence that I thought was needed to go through this process. The next instruction was to find myself within a hallway. My hallway looked like one from a historical hotel; it was long and dingy. The first thing that captured my focus was bright flames at the end of the hallway. These flames seemed to be contained to the end of the hallway. There was no fear that they would move close to me. It was as if there was an invisible barrier between myself and the fire. Although I was fixated on this inferno, I did not communicate it to Denise. Instead, I focused on her next instruction which was to choose one door within the hallway that I would enter. This door would lead to one of my last lives. Even though I was intrigued to move forward and see one of my last lives, it took every amount of effort I could muster to try to do this. I found my door and described it in detail. It was a very generic wood door with a tarnished brass knob. It was a dark colored wood that was not making a great impression on me but I wanted to see what was waiting me on the other side. I pushed the door open and closed it behind me. I found myself in a very small apartment that did not project much comfort or warmth. There was little light other than what was creeping through the closed blinds. There was no one else there; I obviously lived alone. "How are you dressed," Denise asked. I described that I was wearing laced brown shoes and a brown suit. I was balding and wore circular, wire-rimmed glasses. I had the feeling that I was some type of salesman and was returning home from work. The entirety of my vision, with the exception of one part, was colorless like I was the star of a nineteen twenties black and white movie. This exception I spoke of was that fire. All I wanted to do was leave the apartment and return to the hallway to be near the fire. I remember the pressing feeling of needing to share this detail that I had excluded earlier.

I eventually expressed my need to return to the hallway. "The far end of the hallway was engulfed in flames," I told Denise. I explained that it was all I could focus on and had little interest in the door. I felt little attachment to the solitary life I had led within that apartment and wanted to return to the fiery hallway. Her voice asked me to explore what this fire was and why I was so fixated on it. I really had no idea what the answer to this was. Did I die in a fire at the end of that life? Was it representing some type of trauma from childhood that I had repressed? I really was confused by it but I was uncontrollably drawn to it.

Since Denise, nor I, knew what this vision meant, she asked if any of my spirit guides were present to help explain our confusion. We all have many spirit guides and angels that are always by our side to assist us when needed. I focused on this task and was surprisingly successful. I saw a circular portal in front of me. All of a sudden, a very small, video game/cartoon Jesus leaped through this portal. I explained that there was a guide that had appeared to me. Denise asked me to describe what this guide looked like. I remember being so hesitant to say it out loud. "He has long brown hair and a white robe," I said. Let me explain my hesitancy. I am not religious in any way, shape, or form. I have read so many NDE descriptions of encountering a religious figure such as Jesus. I never in a thousand years would have thought I would encounter such a figure in any experience. The difference in the Jesus that I saw and the stories I had read about was that mine was hilariously perfect. My guide chose to present a sense of humor by appearing as an eight bit cartoon which made me laugh so hard. I still laugh about it every time it pops into my head.

The next question that was asked of me was to ask this animated guide how we should refer to him; what was his name? In my vision, I looked at him and asked. I knew that this was a ridiculous question and so did he. Names and titles had no importance to him nor I in this situation. We both new this to be the case but he obliged by offering a name. "My name is I," he simply stated. Again, just as his humorous appearance, his name was perfect. Denise had me ask him about the significance of the fire. His answer was, "he is not ready to know." Denise then instructed me to ask, when will he be ready to know this answer. "He will know when he is ready to know."

Following this message from "I," I was asked to witness the retirement period within this lifetime. I could see myself somewhere in the mountains attempting to escape the hustle and bustle of the big city I had been surviving in. It felt as though I had spent much of that lifetime alone and unhappy. Apparently, my only idea to find some joyous end cap was to seek the quiet beauty of nature. It still appeared to be a very lonely existence up until the actual end.

One last day needed to be sought out to show me the completion to this life: my last day. I witnessed myself as an old man laying on a hospital bed. That was only one of two times I saw a smile upon that previous life's face. The first was upon the arrival to the big city to begin my happy adulthood, which of course did not pan out. This old and frail man that had been me was more than ecstatic to exit this dismal lifetime and move on. The moment of my last breath led to a wonderful ball of light exiting and speeding away at a tremendous rate. My soul had moved on and never looked back. That concluded my view of one of many past lives that I have lived. I was left with only one question: what was the meaning of that colorful fire that I was so fixated on? That answer came much sooner than I had expected. Driving home from my appointment, it hit me; that fire was a different past life of mine. It seemed that it was one full of joy, passion, and happiness, hence why I was so drawn to it. Later that night, I excitedly sent a message to Denise to let her know about my realization. Her reaction was, "WOW!" She was just as excited as I was and said, "we definitely need to do this again to take a look at that life!"

Regress Toward Your Future

One of the major reasons I wanted to experience a past life regression was to show other types of evidence that we all are, at our core, a soul that lives numerous lives. All of the near death experiences that I have documented in this book are very strong evidence to me but there was definitely something to what I had seen in my experience. There can be many ways to show the presence of a soul. I have pursued and documented a variety of different types for this book.

I'm definitely a person who has appreciation for the past but do not believe we should exist within that past. I truly believe in the importance of living in the moment and moving forward into the future. After all, our free will and gut feelings can steer positivity into our future. There are many lessons that can be learned by reviewing our past though. We have all made many mistakes throughout life that maybe we wish we could go back and have a redo. There aren't any do overs, however there are second chances and these second chances offer each one of us the opportunity to not make the same mistakes twice.

I have made mistakes throughout my forty-six years on this planet. I can look back on them and see them with great clarity. Although I cannot change them, I can make sure that I do not make them again. Everyone of us is born into this life free of mistakes, but we quickly begin to accumulate them as we grow older. Take a minute to sit and think about your mistakes. To clarify, think about mistakes that you believe you have made. Do not necessarily focus on mistakes that others have said you have made. Yes, others can, at times, see things that you are unable to see and this can give you another perspective into your life. This is not what I am saying. What I am saying, is sometimes, in certain relationships, others like to project their own issues onto us and point out mistakes that are not really mistakes on our part. There may be moments, in the duration of a relationship, when we attempt to please our significant other; this can lead to losing ourself to please the other person. I can personally say that I have done this and it led to my partner believing that I had made a mistake and that I had failed them. I had given my all to please another and it did nothing but create ill will between us. This was not a mistake, it was an act of love and an attempt to create a happy relationship. Try to remember that if you find yourself in a situation that is similar, you may want to step back and reevaluate yourself and your relationship. Now, back to my question, what do you believe have been your life's greatest mistakes? Take this time to be completely vulnerable to admit your mistakes. After all, vulnerability is the key to a happy life and happy relationships.

My past life regression showed me a major lesson that I need to learn. I am about to reveal my own vulnerability to the world by forever cementing it upon these pages. If I can do it, you can too! The past life that I saw was one of solitude and unhappiness. In that life, I never allowed anyone into my life and spent all of my years alone. I also led a life without joy or passion. I continued on, day in and day out, in a profession that I despised instead of pursuing paths that would have provided happiness. In my current life, I have always followed my creative passions, however, I have, prior to four years ago, let an unlimited amount of people into my life. I always sought out relationships regardless of whether they were healthy ones or not. Recently, I have no desire for a relationship. I hate to say it but the thought of it almost makes me cringe. I have, at this time, lost my faith in the traditional relationship. This does make me sad and I am hoping this feeling is temporary. Currently, my only desire is to focus on my kids and on the things in life that make me truly happy. I have begun to shut out any possibility of having a relationship. My oldest son always tells me, "we aren't always going to be here." Every time he says this, it really makes me think that I am making a mistake; a mistake that I am trying to correct. The past life that I witnessed is showing me that I need to somehow find a happy balance between a life of solitude and a life that is shared with another individual. I do have to say that I am truly happy for the first time in my life. Now that I have found my happiness, I need to allow that special person into my life that will appreciate my individual happiness and will want to add their happiness to create an amazing union that equates to two smiles on a daily basis. There is a middle ground between solitude and relationship overload; I just need to reconcile with this middle ground and open myself up to possibilities. So there you have it, my vulnerability served up on a silver platter for the world to read. I truly hope that maybe it will help at least one person open up about what is holding them back from happiness.

Enough about me and my mistakes, how can you make your life a realization that can bring progress to your existence? It is easier than you think it is. Just allow your protective walls to come down and let the vulnerability flow. Do not let your human ego get in the way of showing your own vulnerability. Honestly, that is all that it takes. Once you allow yourself to do this, you will be shocked at the progress you will achieve and you will find yourself soaring into a happy future of unlimited possibilities.

The Conclusion

Concluding a book, especially one where I am telling the life-changing experiences of incredible people, is almost as challenging as writing an entire book. Placing a bookend on a something like this is a very fun challenge. For the last year I have searched for people who would be interested in sharing their amazing testimonies. I spoke with them and came as close as possible to attempt to feel what they felt and to see what they saw. I wasn't really close at all because these weren't my experiences but as I said, I gave it my all. Although this is true, after each and every one of these conversations, I did feel more alive than ever. I felt the passion and excitement that they each were expressing. It was incredible. I know that I will remember the details of these encounters for the rest of my life. I will not only remember their words, but I will remember the feeling I had at the end of each of them; I felt alive and invigorated. I felt like an angel had touched me and evolved me. I truly hope that all of their words made an evolutionary imprint upon your soul.

My first interview was with Ray Reyes on January 10, 2021. This was the first amazing domino that set the rest in motion. A succession of truthful and non-black and white dominoes that created a beautiful gray dust when they fell. When I hung up the phone I was floating on a cloud of happiness. That afternoon I took my kids sledding and had such an appreciation for everything that I encountered from that day on. We had gone sledding many times prior but that day was different. It was filled with colors and feelings that I will never forget. Everyday since has been filled with the same vibrancy. Appreciation is something that so many human beings do not possess and I'm sure that there have been points in my life where I didn't either. Those points will never be able to creep into my life ever again. The volume has been turned up to eleven when it comes to my appreciation for life and death. They are a beautifully balanced scale of necessity and importance. I feel like a child walking in between the two; both of my hands are holding on tight to both of them. I am forever swinging with each of them holding onto me with all of their strength.

If I posed the following questions to you, what would be your response? What is life? This question seems like it would be very simple to answer doesn't it? When you delve in deep, it's not so easy to answer. Is the answer, to exist within a physical body? That seems far too basic of an answer to me. What if you were laying in a coma with no brain activity and being kept alive by machines? Technically, we would be existing within a physical body, yet we are not experiencing, quote unquote, life in the traditional sense. Now, here is the other question I have for you, what is death? Again, this seams like a quite simplistic question to answer. For me, this is only a physical question and concept. The body does die; this is a one-hundred percent fact. Everyone knows this to be true, therefore I do not need to convince you of this. You know that you will die just as I know that I will.

Now let's discuss that other part of our existence, the soul. I truly hope that by this point you are beginning to believe in the true possibility of a soul. We are not just a simple, chance in a million, bag of bones that is thrusted upon this planet for no apparent reason. Our lives, our amazing and life-sustaining planet, and the infinite beauty of the universe are not just a lucky roll of the dice. There is so much more to it all than we could ever know. The soul is a thread between life and death and it maneuvers its existence through an earthly life and an etheric one. I have never believed in anything as strongly as I do about the factuality of the soul. Belief is an amazing thing. Some believe in Jesus while others believe in the philosophical words of Siddhartha. Some believe in the absence of belief. Today, the masses seem to be leaning towards a belief in materialism (if you want to hear my opinion on this subject, my next book will be for you). Like I said, belief is a very powerful possession. There were definitely times in my life where I did not possess much belief. I can remember when I was much younger and almost relished in the concept of non-belief, although it did not last long. Then, I found love which became a true sacred belief for me. After my one brush with love, I stumbled upon the truest of true loves: having children. To this day, that is my love of loves. I am amazed by this love everyday. I am also amazed on a daily basis by my belief in the soul. I have an all-encompassing awe of the soul. The incredible journey that it embarks on and all of the amazing attributes that it possesses is nothing short of, WOW.

To think that we are all just a physical mass, although a highly complex mass, just does not make sense to me. We are all so much more. Your life and my life are not just a one-shot, make the best of it scenario. Our soul is on a long journey of learning and experiencing while having many ups and downs as we each stumble and soar. Please know that you will definitely soar but also please understand that you will not only stumble, you will fall. You will fall hard many times just as I have fallen quite a few times. This is the great thing to keep in mind, even though the falls hurt really badly at the time, they strengthen us. Those moments of struggle and hardship are, in actuality, the golden moments that teach us and also help us to appreciate the soaring moments.

So, the whole point of this book was to help ease the fear of death by sharing testimonies of individuals who have had near death experiences. I, myself have never had one of these experiences but I feel as though I have. I cannot begin to explain the power of these experiences. If you have doubt that these stories are true, and I can understand the hesitation to believe in their truth, I will convey to you that they are one-hundred percent true. When I spoke to each and every one of these incredible people, I was completely enthralled with the excitement in their voices. They all had, what I can only explain as a tone of purity with each and every word that they uttered. Even the experiences that were beyond traumatic, had a pure silver lining that splashed onto these pages. The silver lining is all that matters. Every moment, although many times difficult to see, has a silver lining. Never, ever forget that.

Life is half full and our physical death is just as full. There is absolutely no reason to have a fear of death. Death is just as beautiful as life. Cherish the journey……

-There is one thing to always remember…death is equally as beautiful as life
  -Approach death as you would a best friend
  -A best friend that will always be there waiting to comfort you

-Me

Death is the ultimate and most joyous surprise party that you could ever imagine

- Me

A letter to Source

I know that, deep within me, you are true and I look forward to seeing you once again. My daily life sometimes attempts to make you a falsehood but I know. I will continue to forge forward one physical step at a time to learn my lessons. I will treat this lifetime like that of an infinite fountain of knowledge that will only result in prosperity and enlightenment. You are my beginning and end that gets me started and greets me at the end of my marathon. You are beautiful in all that you are. You are only truthful purity. You are the wisdom that my mind cannot comprehend.

I will see you when I see you……

www.ingramcontent.com/pod-product-compliance
Lightning Source LLC
Chambersburg PA
CBHW030911080526
44589CB00010B/257